THE GLASS CONSTELLATION

BOOKS BY ARTHUR SZE

POETRY

The Glass Constellation: New and Collected Poems

Sight Lines

Compass Rose

The Ginkgo Light

Quipu

The Redshifting Web: Poems 1970–1998

Archipelago

River River

Dazzled

Two Ravens

The Willow Wind

TRANSLATIONS

The Silk Dragon: Translations from the Chinese

EDITOR

Chinese Writers on Writing

Arthur Sze

THE GLASS CONSTELLATION

NEW AND COLLECTED POEMS

COPPER CANYON PRESS
PORT TOWNSEND, WASHINGTON

Printed in the United States of America

Cover art: Barbara Takenaga, *Clearing,* 2018. Acrylic on linen, 35.75 × 38 inches. Courtesy of DC Moore Gallery.

Copper Canyon Press is in residence at Fort Worden State Park in Port Townsend, Washington, under the auspices of Centrum. Centrum is a gathering place for artists and creative thinkers from around the world, students of all ages and backgrounds, and audiences seeking extraordinary cultural enrichment.

LIBRARY OF CONGRESS CATALOGING-IN-PUBLICATION DATA

Names: Sze, Arthur, author.
Title: The glass constellation : new and collected poems / Arthur Sze.
Description: Port Townsend, Washington : Copper Canyon Press, [2021] |
Summary: "A collection of poems by Arthur Sze"— Provided by publisher.
Identifiers: LCCN 2020047966 | ISBN 9781556596216 (hardback)
Subjects: LCGFT: Poetry.
Classification: LCC PS3569.Z38 G53 2021 | DDC 811/.54—dc23
LC record available at https://lccn.loc.gov/2020047966

98765432 first printing

COPPER CANYON PRESS
Post Office Box 271
Port Townsend, Washington 98368
www.coppercanyonpress.org

for Carol

CONTENTS

FROM *Two Ravens* (1976)

Dazzled (1982)

Archipelago
(1995)

Quipu
(2005)

The Ginkgo Light (2009)

I

II

III

Compass Rose
(2014)

Sight Lines (2019)

The White Orchard: New Poems

THE GLASS CONSTELLATION

OPENING POEMS FROM *The Redshifting Web*

1998

Before Completion

1

I gaze through a telescope at the Orion Nebula,
a blue vapor with a cluster of white stars,
gaze at the globular cluster in Hercules,
needle and pinpoint lights stream into my eyes.
A woman puts a baby in a plastic bag
and places it in a dumpster; someone
parking a car hears it cry and rescues it.
Is this the little o, the earth?
Deer at dusk are munching apple blossoms;
a green snake glides down flowing acequia water.
The night is rich with floating pollen;
in the morning, we break up the soil
to prepare for corn. Fossilized cotton pollen
has been discovered at a site above six thousand feet.
As the character *yi,* change, is derived
from the skin of a chameleon, we are
living the briefest hues on the skin
of the world. I gaze at the Sombrero Galaxy
between Corvus and Spica: on a night with no moon,
I notice my shadow by starlight.

2

Where does matter end and space begin?

blue jays eating suet;

juggling three crumpled newspaper balls
wrapped with duct tape;

tasseling corn;

the gravitational bending of light;

"We're dying";

stringing a coral necklace;

he drew his equations on butcher paper;

vanishing in sunlight;

sobbing;

she folded five hundred paper cranes and placed them in a basket;

sleeping in his room in a hammock;

they drew a shell to represent zero;

red persimmons;

what is it like to catch up to light?

he threw Before Completion:
six in the third place, nine in the sixth.

3

A wavering line of white-faced ibises,
flying up the Rio Grande, disappears.
A psychic says, "Search a pawnshop

for the missing ring." Loss, a black hole.
You do not intend to commit a series of
blunders, but to discover in one error

an empty cocoon. A weaver dumps
flashlight batteries into a red-dye bath.
A physicist says, "After twenty years,

nothing is as I thought it would be."
You recollect watching a yellow-
and-black-banded caterpillar in a jar

form a chrysalis: in days the chrysalis
lightened and became transparent:
a monarch emerged and flexed its wings.

You are startled to retrieve what you forgot:
it has the crunching sound of river
breakup when air is calm and very clear.

4

Beijing, 1985: a poet describes herding pigs
beside a girl with a glass eye and affirms
the power to dream and transform. Later,
in exile, he axes his wife and hangs himself.
Do the transformations of memory
become the changing lines of divination?
Is the continuum of a moment a red
poppy blooming by a fence, or is it
a woman undergoing radiation treatment
who stretches out on a bed to rest
and senses she is stretching out to die?
At night I listen to your breathing,
guess at the freckles on your arms,
smell your hair at the back of your neck.
Tiger lilies are budding in pots in the patio;
daikon is growing deep in the garden.
I see a bewildered man ask for direction,
and a daikon picker points the way with a daikon.

5

He threw Duration;

sunspots;

what is it like to catch up to light?

a collapsing vertebra;

the folding wings of a blue damselfly;

receiving a fax;

buffeted on a floatplane between islands;

a peregrine falcon making a slow circle with outstretched wings;

he crumpled papers, threw them on the floor,
called it City of Bums;

polar aligning;

inhaling the smell of her hair;

a red handprint on a sandstone wall;

digging up ginseng;

carding wool;

where does matter end and space begin?

6

Mushroom hunting at the ski basin, I spot
a bloodred amanita pushing up under fir,
find a white-gilled Man On Horseback,
notice dirt breaking and carefully unearth
a cluster of gold chanterelles. I stop
and gaze at yellow light in a clearing.
As grief dissolves and the mind begins to clear,
an s twist begins to loosen the z-twisted fiber.
A spider asleep under a geranium leaf
may rest a leg on the radial string of a web,
but cool nights are pushing nasturtiums to bloom.
An eggplant deepens in hue and drops to the ground.
Yellow specks of dust float in the clearing;
in memory, a series of synchronous spaces.
As a cotton fiber burns in an s twist
and unravels the z twist of its existence,
the mind unravels and ravels a wave of light,
persimmons ripening on leafless trees.

The String Diamond

1

An apricot blossom opens to five petals.
You step on a nail, and, even as you wince,
a man closes a mailbox, a cook sears
shredded pork in a wok, a surgeon sews
a woman up but forgets to remove a sponge.
In the waiting room, you stare at a diagram
and sense compression of a nerve where
it passes through the wrist and into the hand.
You are staring at black and white counters
on a crisscrossed board and have no idea
where to begin. A gardener trims chamisa
in a driveway; a roofer mops hot tar;
a plumber asphyxiates in a room with
a faulty gas heater; a mechanic becomes
an irrational number and spirals into himself.
And you wonder what inchoate griefs
are beginning to form? A daykeeper sets
a random handful of seeds and crystals into lots.

2

Pin a mourning cloak to a board and observe
brown in the wings spreading out to a series

of blue circles along a cream-yellow outer band.
A retired oceanographer remembers his father

acted as a double agent during the Japanese occupation,
but the Guomindang general who promised a pardon

was assassinated; his father was later sentenced
as a collaborator to life in prison, where he died.

Drinking snake blood and eating deer antler
is no guarantee the mind will deepen and glow.

You notice three of the four corners of an intersection
are marked by ginkgo, horse chestnut, cluster

of pear trees, and wonder what the significance is.
Is the motion of a red-dye droplet descending

in clear water the ineluctable motion of a life?
The melting point of ice is a point of transparency,

as is a kiss, or a leaf beginning to redden,
or below a thunderhead lines of rain vanishing in air.

3

Deltoid spurge,
red wolf,
ocelot,
green-blossom pearlymussel,
razorback sucker,
wireweed,
blunt-nosed leopard lizard,
mat-forming quillwort,
longspurred mint,
kern mallow,
Schaus swallowtail,
pygmy madtom,
relict trillium,
tan riffleshell,
humpback chub,
large-flowered skullcap,
black lace cactus,
tidewater goby,
slender-horned spineflower,
sentry milk-vetch,
tulotoma snail,
rice rat,
blowout penstemon,
rough pigtoe,
marsh sandwort,
snakeroot,
scrub plum,
bluemask darter,
crested honeycreeper,
rough-leaved loosestrife.

4

In the mind, an emotion dissolves into a hue;
there's the violet haze when a teen drinks
a pint of paint thinner, the incarnadined
when, by accident, you draw a piece of
Xerox paper across your palm and slit
open your skin, the yellow when you hear
they have dug up a four-thousand-year-old
corpse in the Taklamakan Desert,
the scarlet when you struggle to decipher
a series of glyphs which appear to
represent sunlight dropping to earth
at equinoctial noon, there's the azure
when the acupuncturist son of a rabbi
extols the virtues of lentils, the brown
when you hear a man iced in the Alps
for four thousand years carried dried
polypores on a string, the green when
ravens cry from the tops of swaying spruces.

5

The first leaves on an apricot, a new moon,
a woman in a wheelchair smoking in a patio,
a CAT scan of a brain: these are the beginnings
of strings. The pattern of black and white
stones never repeats. Each loss is particular:
a gold ginkgo leaf lying on the sidewalk,
the room where a girl sobs. A man returns
to China, invites an old friend to dinner,
and later hears his friend felt he missed
the moment he was asked a favor and was
humiliated; he tells others never to see
this person from America, "He's cunning, ruthless."
The struggle to sense a nuance of emotion
resembles a chrysalis hanging from a twig.
The upstairs bedroom filling with the aroma
of lilies becomes a breathing diamond.
Can a chrysalis pump milkweed toxins into wings?
In the mind, what never repeats? Or repeats endlessly?

6

Dropping circles of gold paper,
before he dies,
onto Piazza San Marco;

    pulling a U-turn
    and throwing the finger;

a giant puffball
filling the car
with the smell of almonds;

    a daykeeper pronounces the day,
    "Net";

slits a wrist,
writes the characters *revolt*
in blood on a white T-shirt;

    a dead bumblebee
    in the greenhouse;

the flaring tail of a comet,
desiccated vineyard,
tsunami;

    a ten-dimensional
    form of go;

slicing abalone on the counter—
sea urchins
piled in a Styrofoam box;

    honeydew seeds
    germinating in darkness.

7

A hummingbird alights on a lilac branch
and stills the mind. A million monarchs
may die in a frost? I follow the wave
of blooming in the yard: from iris to
wild rose to dianthus to poppy to lobelia
to hollyhock. You may find a wave in
a black-headed grosbeak singing from a cottonwood
or in listening to a cricket at dusk.
I inhale the smell of your hair and see
the cloud of ink a cuttlefish releases in water.
You may find a wave in a smoked and
flattened pig's head at a Chengdu market,
or in the diamond pulse of a butterfly.
I may find it pulling yarn out of an indigo vat
for the twentieth time, watching the yarn
turn dark, darker in air. I find it
with my hand along the curve of your waist,
sensing in slow seconds the tilt of the Milky Way.

Kaiseki

1

An aunt has developed carpal tunnel syndrome
from using a pipette. During the Cultural Revolution,
she was tortured with sleep deprivation. Some
of the connections in her memory dissolved
into gaps. "My mind has leaps now," she says,
as she reaches for bean threads in a boiling pot.
Her son recollects people lined up to buy
slices of cancerous tripe. "If you boil it,
it's edible," he says. And a couple who ate
a destroying angel testified it was delicious—
they had not intended to become love suicides.
What are the points of transformation in a life?
You choose three green Qianlong coins and throw
Corners of the Mouth, with no changing lines.
You see red and green seaweed washing onto
smooth black stones along a rocky shoreline,
sense the moment when gravity overtakes light
and the cosmos stops expanding and begins to contract.

2

In the Brazos, he has never found a matsutake
under ponderosa pine, but in the dark

he whiffs it pungent white. Five votive candles
are lined along the fireplace; she has lit

a new candle even though the one burning
holds days of light. The night-blooming cereus

by the studio window is budding from rain.
In his mind, he sees the flyswatter

hanging from a nail on the lintel, a two-eyed
Daruma hanging from the rearview mirror of the car.

He hears the dipping-and-rising pitch of a siren
glide up the street and senses a shift

in starlight, the Horsehead Nebula, and, in the dark,
her eyelashes closing and opening on his skin.

3

He knew by the sound that the arrow was going to miss the target;

pins floating on water;

I saw the collapsing rafters in flames;

the dark side of the moon;

if *p* then *q;*

simplicity is to complexity
as a photon is to a hummingbird?

fire turns to what is dry;

when the Chinese woman wore a blond wig,
people grew uneasy;

an egg exploding in a microwave;

morels pushing up through burned ground;

at the cash register,
Siamese fighting fish were stacked in small glass bowls;

she lost all her hair;

digging up truffles;

what is "a quantum unit of light"?

4

Tokpela: sky: the first world; in her mind,
she has designed an exhibit exemplifying
Hopi time and space. He sees the white sash
with knots and strands hanging from the *trastero.*
He sees the wild rose by the gate,
red nasturtiums blooming by the kitchen door.
She is pressing the blender button and grinding
cochineal bugs into bits; she is sorting
slides of Anasazi textile fragments on a light board.
He recalls when they let loose a swarm
of ladybugs in the yard. It is light-years
since she wove a white manta on the vertical loom,
light-years since they walked out together
to the tip of Walpi and saw the San Francisco Peaks.
Goldfish swim in the pond in the back garden.
The night-blooming cereus opens five white blossoms
in a single night. He remembers looking
through a telescope at craters, and craters
inside craters on the moon. He recalls
being startled at the thought, gravity precedes light.

5

They searched and searched for a loggerhead shrike;

"I can't believe how you make me come"—
she knew he was married
but invited him to the opera;

diving for sea urchins;

the skin of a stone;

"You asshole!"

the nuclear trigrams were identical;

the wing beats of a crow;

maggots were crawling inside the lactarius cap;
for each species of mushroom,
a particular fly;

a broad-tailed hummingbird
whirred at an orange nasturtium;

"Your time has come";

opening the shed with a batten;

p if and only if *q;*

he put the flyswatter back on the nail.

6

The budding chrysanthemums in the jar have the color
of dried blood. Once, as she lit a new candle,

he asked, "What do you pray for?" and remembered
her earlobe between his teeth but received a gash

when she replied, "Money." He sees the octagonal
mirror at a right angle to the fuse box, sees

the circular mirror nailed into the bark of the elm
at the front gate and wonders why the obsession

with feng shui. He recalls the photograph of a weaver
at a vertical loom kneeling at an unfinished

Two Grey Hills and wonders, is she weaving or unweaving?
The candlelight flickers at the bottom of the jar.

He sees back to the millisecond the cosmos was pure energy
and chooses to light a new candle in her absence.

7

I plunge enoki mushrooms into simmering broth
and dip them in wasabi, see a woman remove
a red-hot bowl from a kiln and smother it in sawdust.
I see a right-hand petroglyph with concentric
circles inside the palm, and feel I am running
a scrap of metal lath across a drying coat of cement.
I eat sea urchin roe and see an orange starfish
clinging below the swaying waterline to a rock.
I am opening my hands to a man who waves
an eagle feather over them, feel the stretch
and stretch of a ray of starlight. This
black raku bowl with a lead-and-stone glaze
has the imprint of tongs. I dip raw blowfish
into simmering sake on a brazier, see a lover
who combs her hair and is unaware she is humming.
I see a girl crunching on chips at the Laundromat,
sense the bobbing red head of a Mexican finch.
Isn't this the most mysterious of all possible worlds?

8

A heated stone on a white bed of salt—

sleeping on a subway grate—

a thistle growing in a wash—

sap oozing out the trunk of a plum—

yellow and red roses hanging upside down under a skylight—

fish carcasses at the end of a spit—

two right hands on a brush drawing a dot then the character, *water*—

an ostrich egg—

a coyote trotting across the street in broad daylight—

sharpening a non-photo blue pencil—

the scar at a left wrist—

a wet sycamore leaf on the sidewalk—

lighting a kerosene lamp on a float house—

kaiseki: breast stones: a Zen meal—

setting a yarrow stalk aside to represent the infinite—

9

They threw Pushing Upward—

the pearl on a gold thread dangling at her throat—

a rice bowl with a splashed white slip—

biting the back of her neck—

as a galaxy acts as a gravitational lens and bends light—

stirring *matcha* to a froth with a bamboo whisk—

brushing her hair across his body—

noticing a crack
has been repaired with gold lacquer—

Comet Hyakutake's tail flaring upward in the April sky—

orange and pink entwined bougainvilleas blooming in a pot—

"Oh god, oh my god," she whispered and began to glow—

yellow tulips opening into daylight—

staring at a black dot on the brown iris of her right eye—

water flows to what is wet.

Apache Plume

1 The Beginning Web

Blue flax blossoming near the greenhouse
is a luminous spot, as is a point south

of the Barrancas where two rivers join.
By the cattail pond, you hear dogs

killing a raccoon. In mind, these spots
breathe and glow. In the bath I pour

water over your shoulder, notice the spot
where a wild leaf has grazed your skin.

I see the sun drop below the San Andres
Mountains, white dunes in starlight;

in the breathing chiaroscuro, I glimpse
red-winged blackbirds nesting in the cattails,

see a cow pushing at the wobbly point
in a fence. In this beginning web of light,

I feel the loops and whorls of your fingertips,
hear free-tailed bats swirling out into the dark.

2 Reductions and Enlargements

A Chippewa designer dies from pancreatic cancer
and leaves behind tracing paper, X-Acto knives,

rubber cement, non-photo blue pencils,
a circular instrument that calculates reductions

and enlargements. A child enters a house and finds
a dead man whose face has been eaten by dogs.

Who is measuring the pull of the moon in a teacup?
In a thousand years, a man may find barrels

of radioactive waste in a salt bed and be unable
to read the warnings. Sand is accumulating

at the bottom of an hourglass, and anything—
scissors, green wind chime, pencil shavings,

eraser smudge, blooming orchid under skylight—
may be a radial point into light. When a carp

flaps its tail and sends ripples across the surface
of a pond, my mind steadies into a glow. Look

at a line that goes into water, watch the wake,
see the string pulse and stretch into curved light.

3 The Names of a Bird

You find a downy woodpecker on the bedroom floor.
I am startled and listen in the snowy dark

to deer approach a house and strip yew leaves.
In pots, agapanthuses are opening umbels

of violet flowers. Neither driven by hunger
nor flowering in the moment, what drives an oologist

to distinguish finch eggs from wren or sparrow?
What drives a physicist to insist the word

sokol means *falcon* in Hungarian? If you know
the names of a bird in ten languages, do you know

any more about the bird? Driving past an ostrich farm,
I recollect how you folded a desert willow blossom

into a notebook; I recollect rolling down
a white dune at dusk, pulling a green jade disk

on a thread at your throat into my mouth.
I know what it is to touch the mole between your breasts.

4 The Architecture of Silence

The gate was unlocked. We drove to the road's end; grapefruit lay on the ground not far from a white house whose window caught a glare. December 29, four p.m. At first we couldn't find the trail but walked ahead and crossed a river full of black boulders. Days earlier, we had looked down into the valley from a *kukui* grove. There was speckled bark, slanting rain, horses in a field, drenching rain. We had been walking back from the ocean where we moved from rock to rock and saw black crabs scuttling along the tide line. We looked into the water, saw sea cucumbers on rocks. On the way back, white lepiotas among grass and a small white puffball. I sliced open the puffball, but it was olive-green. Deer, crossing the road, stopped near the fence line and gazed back at us. I inhaled the aroma of shredded ginger and saw three pairs of dragonflies overhead, their wings catching daylight. Where is the one inside the many? Or are there many inside one? We came to a fork in the trail and noticed an exposed root growing across the right branch. We twisted left and glimpsed twin waterfalls; wild boar were stunned in our headlights. In the twilight, we came to another stream with white water rushing across black boulders and paused:

raindrops
dropping off the eaves
stop dropping

5 Hourglass

Père Lachaise: breaking bread on a green bench
under chestnut trees as rain drizzles down the leaves
and smoke rises out of the crematorium chimney—

is recollection a form of memento mori?
I see papyrus growing in a copper tub in the bedroom;
your hands rub blackthorn oil into my skin.

I close my eyes, feel the warmth of straw-flecked adobe walls—
a white chrysanthemum opens in a cup of boiling water.
Willow leaves on the skylight cast onto an ochre wall

shadows resembling herring under a float house.
Is recollection a form of epistemological inquiry?
I am cradling you as you lean back into me,

flecks of white sand in your hair and on your eyelids.
I am holding you in a white dune as the moon rises,
as white sand begins to touch the bottom of an hourglass.

6 Entelechy

Placing long-stemmed sunflowers in a vase
or staring at a map of Paris

may be a form of ripening.
In the garden, red-leaf lettuce has bolted in the heat.

The surface of water in an old whiskey barrel
twitches with mosquito larvae.

A bingo billboard on a highway
may be a momentary rippling,

but the deeper undulation is shark-womb skin.
Slicing abalone on the counter,

I catch a tidal surge at my fingertips.
By candlelight, a yellow cosmos,

koi roiling the surface of a stream into gold flecks,
your sharp wild cries.

7 Apache Plume

Climbing out of an arroyo, I reach my hand
into a small cactus and see the taro

plant in the backyard unfurl a new leaf.
A great horned owl perched on a ledge

twitches its ears when we approach along
the bottom of a ravine. I spot a hummingbird

at the hollyhock, pear blossoms swirling
on gravel near the gate. When you light

a candle, the flickering shadow on the wall
has the shape of an eagle feather.

In the morning when you do a yoga stretch,
I feel the rhythm with which you sway—

fingertip to fingertip, mouth to mouth,
the shifting course of the Pojoaque River,

white apache plume blossoming to silvery puff.
And as an astronomer catches light echoes

from a nova, when I pull spines out of my palm,
I know this instant moment which is ours.

8 Anamnesis

Wind erases our footprints on a transverse dune.
A yellow yolk of sun drops below the horizon

as a white moon rises. Claret cup cactus
blooms in white sand, while soaptree yuccas

move as a dune moves. The mind reduces a pond
to a luminous green speck and enlarges

a flecked *Amanita muscaria* cap into a cosmos.
Running my hand along the curve of your waist,

I wonder if knowledge is a form of anamnesis.
When I pour warm water down your spine,

a *Boletus barrowsii* releases spores into air.
As a stone drops into a pool and red koi

swim toward the point of impact, we set
a yarrow stalk aside and throw Duration,

glimpse a spiral of bats ascending out of a cave;
one by one they flare off into indigo air.

9 Starlight

Here skid marks on I-25 mark a head-on collision;

here I folded an origami crane;

here a man writes in grass style: *huan wo he shan;*

here black poplar leaves swayed on the surface of clearest water;

here a downy woodpecker drills high in the elm;

here a dog drags a horse's leg back from the arroyo;

here Keene's cement burned into my wrist and formed a riparian scar;

here, traveling at night through the Sonoran Desert,
everyone choked when sand swept through the open windows of the train;

here yellow and red ranunculus unfold under a chandelier;

here in the Jemez Mountains a cluster of *Clitocybe dilatata;*

here we spot eleven dolphins swimming between kelp beds up the coast;

here we look through binoculars at the blue ion tail of a comet in the northwest sky;

here pelicans are gliding above a cliff;

here when I pour water down the drain, a black cricket pops up;

here the first thing I saw when I opened my eyes
was a cut peony in a glass;

here is the origin of starlight.

10 Diffraction Grating

Sipping kava out of a tea bowl,
I am descending into a cavern that inhales

and exhales once each day. I see an alula
in a tropical greenhouse, the tracks

a bleached earless lizard makes in white sand,
the tracks my fingers make on your skin.

I see a spectrum of origami cranes
strung on thread at a Kurashiki temple,

Manchurian cranes in a cage and a salt
sumo ring. Papyrus stalks arc out of an urn

near the fireplace on the bedroom floor.
Is a solar flare a form of koan?

Blue larkspur in a glass vase.
A stalactite dripping into a pool of water.

Hush: there is nothing in ten dimensions
that is not dilating the pupils of our eyes.

Six Persimmons

1

"Cabrón," rings in his ears as he walks down
the corridor to death row. Where is the epicenter
of a Los Angeles earthquake? Hypocenter of Fat Man?
He watches a woman pour honey into a jar crammed
with psilocybin mushrooms. A few cells down,
a priest intones and oozes black truffles in olive oil.
He is about to look at the poems of a murderer,
sees a sliced five-thousand-year-old silkworm cocoon.
X: pinhole, eclipse; the, a; shadow of mosquito,
fern frond uncoiling in mist. "Dot," says a Japanese
calligrapher who draws a dot beginning on the floor
off the page. He looks at the page, shrugs,
there is nothing there, and pictures budding chamisa
in a courtyard, yellow yarrow hanging over a bed.
In Waimea Canyon, *'apapane, 'i'iwi.* X: it's
the shapes of ice in an ice floe, a light-green
glazed lotus-shaped hot-water bowl. He opens his eyes
and recalls staring into her eyes as she comes.

2

A visual anthropologist dies in a head-on collision
and leaves behind an Okinawan bow, arrows, whisk,
Bizen bowl, hammock, New Guinea coffee beans,
calligraphic scroll, "In motion there is stillness."
Walking along the shifting course of the Pojoaque River,
I ponder the formation of sunspots, how they appear
to be floating islands, gigantic magnetic storms
on the surface of the sun, and, forming cooler regions,
become darker to the human eye. I ponder how
he slowed the very sharpening of a pencil
but sped up La Bajada behind a semi in the dark,
and, when the semi shifted into the right lane,
was sandwiched and smashed into an out-of-state
pickup driving down the wrong side of the highway.
I hold the blued seconds when—Einstein Cross—
he cursed, slammed on the brakes—the car crunched
and flew apart in a noise he could not hear into
a pungent white saguaro blossom opening for a single night.

3

Green dragonflies hover over water. In the mind,
the axis of absence and presence resembles
a lunar eclipse. Hiking a ridge trail in the Barrancas,
we notice the translucent wing feathers of
a red-tailed hawk circling overhead. Once,
inadvertently, I glanced out the bathroom window
and noticed yellow yarrow blooming in sunshine.
A man does not have to gamble his car away
and hitchhike out of Las Vegas for the mind to ripen.
Bill Isaacs slices an agaricus lengthwise, points
to the yellow base of stipe, says, "Xanthodermus."
Although he has walked up a trail into spruce
and fir, mycelium in his hands has spread out.
Although asthma may be passed from one to another,
one mind may be a sieve, while the other may be
crystals growing up a string. Is sun to earth to moon
as mind to shiitake to knife? When one mind
passes to another, green dragonflies hover over water.

4

Is the recollecting mind an aviary? Once he pushed
through hermetically sealed revolving doors
into a humid forest where he sighted a toucan,
but where is the *ʻōʻō ʻaʻa*? A pin fits in a pocket,
but how do you put a world inside a world?
Two twins, ex-marines, stretch Okinawan bows
and aim their hips and eyes at the target;
the arrows are not yet not yet released.
As death burns a hole into a piece of paper,
a fern frond in the Alakaʻi Swamp uncoils in mist.
He glows when she puts her hand on his chest;
the sun spins faster at the equator than at the poles.
He lays six blossoming orchid branches on the floor,
stares at the shapes of flower vases on shelves
in the storeroom. It is as if all the possible shapes
of the world were waiting to come into being,
as if a new shape was about to come into being,
when, x, a calico cat scratches at the door.

5

When you stoop to examine a lichen but find
alongside, barely exposed, several gold chanterelles,
I bend to earth in my mind: observe striations
along a white cap, absence of annulus, dig,
unearth a volva. We go on in the woods
and stumble into a cluster of teeth fungi
with dark upturned scales on their caps.
Who notices in the early morning Saturn slip
behind a waning gibbous moon? This year,
a creation spiral slowly incandesces in my hand.
I slip a white elastic band off and loosen
your hair, rub my thumb in your palm. I love
when wet sunlight splashes your face, recall
grilling shrimp near a corner of the screened porch
while rain slants across the field. In the few
weeks of a year when bloodred amanitas push
out of the earth, we push into a splendor of
yellow plumeria, orange hibiscus, bird-of-paradise.

6

Pears ripen in a lacquer bowl on the butcher-
block table. A red shimmer arcs across
the northwest sky as a galaxy bends the light
of a quasar. Yellow ranunculus unfold in a glass vase
while fireflies blink in a corner of the yard.
A physicist employs lasers and slows atoms
down to approach absolute zero; a calligrapher
draws the silk radical twice, then *mountain,*
to form "the most shady recesses in the hills."
As the ink dries, she lights two red candles
in the bedroom, notices near the curtains
taro in the huge tin tub, and spots a curling leaf.
He hears the gasp when he first unzipped
her jeans, knows the small o is a lotus seed
slowly germinating in his mind, but the
brevity of equation makes him quiver and ache.
When they turn to each other in a wet kiss,
their fingertips glow in the skin of their days.

FROM *The Willow Wind*

1972

Noah's / Dove

The moon is black.
Had I a bird
it would fly,
beat the air into land.
To remain
or trust
the silver leaves of the sea?
What if
I say what *is:*
no bird, no land.
The sea tossing
its damp wet fish
on the bow,
their lungs exhaling
the sea, taking in
moon air
for the first time . . .

The Wood Whittler

Whales and fish
sailing
in the sky!

Old saws! Old saws!
Red flakes
falling off the wood

like leaves.
Fire?
The woodcutter

pares the skin
with a
knowing hand.

The blade—rude—
will carve
his / mind's mastery

in the /
witless earth.

Li Po

Jarred.
    The oars creaked in their locks.
Fish beneath the moon.
Cradled his pen
filled with wine.
        A goddess stirred,
rocked the cradle of his boat,
let the silent fish know
a dreamer's silver hands were at work.

Pegasus on a Pipe

He would ride the moon,
prod the slow seahorse with a cake of salt
and when it broke sweat,
urge it ease,
watch the wings sprout, remorseless.

Miracles

His lens misses her,
the leaves cast double reflections
on the glass. The one
is his shadow; as he leans up
he discovers a new perspective,
a range he never considered.
The leaves, shaggy edged,
twirl the light in their hands.
A new source; he must
pay his respects deftly.
They have his power.
He must acquaint them
with this peripheral vision—
the woman walking down the steps
is no longer his wife.

The Execution of Maximilian

Muskets triggered a white smoke,
and it fell like snow,
soft death to purple eyes.
I saw the clean glint of the man's pants,
and knew what was coming,
hit the ground for the last time.

And the snow covered me like a corpse.
They mistook me for one
who had lain there a long time.
And they rushed on instead
to the crumpled body by the wall,
stuck their bayonets in
laughing, and jostled each other on the shoulder
like friends long unseen, now returned.

Sound Lag

His glazed lips
moved slower
than the
movement of words.
Overhead, black clouds
were poised
in the sky,
then moved on.
In the real sky
they had
no place to go.

The air cooled to zero.
I look again at myself
in the mirror.
The veins of the dark trees
outside
vibrate.
Their song is, at least,
mine, but
I am engaged elsewhere.
I extend my hand
through the glass
into the living world.

Sliding Away

Your hand rigid, curled into its final shape:
the rest of your body breathes.
The dark coals you pour on his grave
continue to breathe.
A snake slides through the
uneven grass
where it has cut a
name for
itself
by
sliding away.

Strawberries in Wooden Bowls

You carry flowers in a jug of green wine,
and the smell is that of the first fires in autumn
when the leaves are blown into their reds and grays.

The sunlight rains through the glass.
As you reach across the table
the fences outside disappear.
The fields are green with their rain
and the wind curls the stars in the cold air.

You stand now, silent, in the window of light
and the milk you pour is glazed.
The strawberries in the wooden bowls
are half-covered with curdled milk.

The Olive Grove

Up on the hill
the morning moon washed clean.
Thin dogs no longer
leap in the sunlight,
and I walk, easily, up the path.
The gatekeeper snores
in his rocking chair,
and only the wind
keeps him moving.

Turning now through the yard
I recall his eyes.
The leaves tinged
with inevitable grays.
With one hand
I pluck the olives
off the white lattice.
Their thick skins
rinsed in the moonshine.

A Singer with Eyes of Sand

A singer with eyes of sand they said—
the western wind
                                        sweeps me home,
and I am carrying you, my desert,
in my hands.

FROM *Two Ravens*

1976

The Taoist Painter

He begins with charcoal and outlines
the yellow fringes of the trees.
Then he rubs in the stumps, black
and brown, with an uneasy motion
of his thumbs. Unlike trees in the north,
he says, I have the option of season.
And he paints the leaves in the upswing
of the wind, and the swans craning their necks.
But the sunlight moving in patches
obscures and clarifies his view.
When he walks off in silence
we look at his painting and stand
astonished to see how, in chiaroscuro,
the leaves drift to their death.

Bruegel

The haystacks burned to black moss.
I tilted my head and leveled
the mound; saw three women walking
home in step, hefting hoes, and
weighted by sunlight on the blades.
Three men, of course, circled away,
heads concealed by hats, joking,
clearly drunk on harvest wine.
But then the pageant slipped off
without me; the horse loped across
the ridge, and the sickle mender
tuned his ears to the wind.

The Silver Trade

You will hammer silver into a heart
and the dogs will leap and yell.
No one will stop you though, and
before learning how the body dies,
you will smelt earrings for fuel.

Nail my spine to wood. I cannot live.
Under the open sky the wind
whips the sunlight into stone.
I thread the few stars into a crown
and throw them behind the mountain.

He Will Come to My Funeral with a White Flower

He will come to my funeral with a white flower
and spread the petals, unevenly, on my dress.
Then he will turn, walk down the aisle, and
raise his elbow to accompany his invisible bride.
Oh, though he comes with me to the market
and we buy fruit and vegetables for dinner,
he is a hermit in the mountains, watching
the water and the sunlight on the green stones.
His hands skim the rise and fall, reshaping
the ridges and making the bend a woman's thigh.
No one can ever be part of his village, don
palm leaves and wear an inscrutable smile.
When he says goodbye, I know the water in his eyes
has been falling for centuries.

Two Ravens

discussed the weather?
or, perhaps, inquired about spring?

Two ravens, lovers, discussed my death
as I watched.

The Waking

Blue plums in the pewter bowl—
may they wake wet in the earth the wren singing
and cull the sweetest violet.
But the children sleep secure in blankets.

I climbed by spinning arms and legs against walls,
awakened waist-deep in the water-well;
wrestled the black bull before an audience,
beat the wind without wings,
paced the steeds along pampas grass . . .

In the morning chill
I breathe moths in my cupped hands.

North to Taos

The aspen twig
    or leaf will snap: bells in the wind,
and the hills, obsidian,
    as the stars wheeling halt;
        twig and bark curling in the fire
kindle clusters of sparks.
    Steer north, then, to Taos, where
        the river, running deeper, cuts a gorge,
    and at midnight the moon
waxes; minnows scatter
    at your step,
        the boat is moored to sky.

Three a.m., in Winter

When I went to Zuni,
    my mind was a singing arrow; the black desert
was shining, and I flew,
    a green peyote bird, in the wind's eye . . .
It's three a.m., and
    the road to Zuni is buried in snow.
        Thinking of you, I taste green wine,
    I touch sparks, I fly.

Lament

Let me pick
olives in the moonlight.
Let me ride
a pale green horse.
Let me taste the autumn fires.
Or else,
let me die in a war.

No Hieroglyphics

No hieroglyphics but the bird singing in the throat of the tree.
When I walk home, my hair bristling, hear you read
by the hearth in slow fire. No calendars
to twist days into years or
months back to seconds.
We live in fear.
But open our
lives to the sea.
Walk on water with the
moon. Stars, stars! No one to
teach. That the long day slips into night.
As the mind withers in the tree. But only to sail
a boat without wind. Down the endless river. The sand running out.

Wang Wei

At my window
    the rain raves, raves about dying,
and does not
    hear in the bamboo
        a zither, which, plucked,
inebriates the birds
    and brings closer to the heart
        the moon.

Morning Shutters

We extend arms
infinitely long
into the sunrise.

Then the shutters close,
and we begin
the slow, painful
step of learning
shadows in the dark.

My hand goes to your thigh.
The hills
high above us
shine in the heat.

Now, the whites of your eyes
are filled
with the lost years.

Lupine

I planted lupine and nasturtiums
in the dark April dirt. Who heard the passing
cars or trucks? I was held

by your face, eclipsed, in partial light.
I sip hibiscus tea, and am at peace
in the purple dusk.

“Kwan, kwan,” cries a bird, distant,
in the pines.

Do Not Speak Keresan to a Mescalero Apache

Do not speak
Keresan to a Mescalero Apache,
but cultivate
private languages;

a cottonwood
as it disintegrates into gold,
or a house
nailed into the earth:

the dirt road
into that reservation
is unmarked.

Dazzled

1982

Viewing Photographs of China

Viewing photographs of China,
we visit a pearl farm, factories, and
watch a woman stare at us ten
minutes after a surgical operation
with acupuncture.
                                        The mind
is a golden eagle. An arctic tern
is flying in the desert: and
the desert incarnadined, the sun
incarnadined.
                                The photograph
of a poster of Chang Ch'ing is
two removes from reality. Lin Piao,
Liu Shao-chi, and Chang Ch'ing
are either dead or disgraced.
The poster shows her in a loose
dress drinking a martini; the
issues of the Cultural Revolution
are confounded.
                                    And, in perusing
the photographs in the mind's eye,
we discern bamboo, factories,
pearls; and consider African wars,
the Russian Revolution, the
Tierra Amarilla Courthouse Raid.
And instead of insisting that
the world have an essence, we
juxtapose, as in a collage,
facts, ideas, images:
                                        the arctic
tern, the pearl farm, considerations
of the two World Wars, Peruvian
horses, executions, concentration
camps; and find, as in a sapphire,
a clear light, a clear emerging
view of the world.

The Moon Is a Diamond

Flavio Gonzales, seventy-two, made jackhammer
heads during the War; and tells me
about digging ditches in the Depression
for a dollar a day. We are busy plastering
the portal, and stop for a moment
in the April sun. His wife, sick for
years, died last January and left a
legacy—a $5,000 hospital bill.
I see the house he built at fifteen:
the *ristras* of red chile hanging
in the October sun. He sings "Paloma
Blanca" as he works, then stops,
turns: "I saw the TV photos of the
landing on the moon. But it's all
lies. The government just went out
in the desert and found a crater.
Believe me, I know, I know the moon
is a diamond."

Listening to a Broken Radio

1

The night is
a black diamond.
I get up at 5:30 to drive to Jemez Pueblo,
and pass the sign at the bank
at 6:04, temperature 37.
And brood: a canyon wren, awake, in its nest in the black pines,
and in the snow.

2

America likes
the TV news that shows you the
great winning catch in a football game.
I turn left
at the Kiska store.
And think of the peripatetic woman
who lives with all her possessions in a shopping cart,
who lives on Sixth Avenue at Eighth Street,
and who prizes and listens to her
broken radio.

Moenkopi

Your father had gangrene and
had his right leg amputated, and now has diabetes
and lives in a house overlooking the
uranium mines.
The wife of the clown at Moenkopi
smashes in the windows of a car with an ax,
and threatens to shoot her husband
for running around with another woman.

A child with broken bones
is in the oxygen tent for the second time;
and the parents are concerned he
has not yet learned how to walk.
People mention these incidents
as if they were points on a chart depicting
uranium disintegration. It is all
accepted, all disclaimed.

We fly a kite over the electrical
lines as the streetlights go on:
the night is silver, and the night
desert is a sea. We walk back
to find your grandfather working in the dark,
putting in a post to protect peaches,
watering tomatoes, corn, beans—making them grow
out of sand, barren sand.

Written the Day I Was to Begin a Residency at the Penitentiary of New Mexico

Inmates put an acetylene torch to another inmate's face,
seared out his eyes.
Others were tortured, lacerated with barbed wire,
knifed, clobbered with lead pipes.

I remember going to the state pen to see a performance of Beckett.
I see two inmates play Hamm and Clov.
Clov lifts weights all day,
his biceps are huge.
And Hamm, in a wheelchair with a bloody handkerchief,
dark purple shades,
is wheeled around and around
in a circle in the gym:
as guards watch, talk on walkie-talkies, slam doors,
as a television crew tapes segments.

I do not know whether these two inmates died or lived.
But they are now the parts they played:
locked in a scenario of bondage and desperate need,
needing each other to define themselves.

I tell myself to be open to all experience,
to take what is ugly and find something nourishing in it:
as penicillin may be found in green moldy bread,
or as, in the morning, a child of the earth
floating in a porcelain jar full of rainwater
is something astonishing.

But after the SWAT team has moved in and taken over
the flotsam and jetsam of a prison,
and the inmates are lined up and handcuffed to a chain-link fence,
I figure their chances, without people caring,
are "an ice cube's chance in hell."

Gold Leaf

Is the sun a miner, a thief, a gambler,
an assassin? We think the world

is a gold leaf spinning down in silence
to clear water? The deer watch us in the blue leaves.

The sun shines in the June river. We flit
from joy to grief to joy as a passing

shadow passes? And we who think the sun a miner,
a thief, a gambler, an assassin,

find the world in a gold leaf spinning down
in silence to clear water.

Dazzled

Reality
is like a contemporary string
quartet:

the first violinist puts on a crow's head.
And the cellist

soliloquizes on a white lotus
in the rain.

The violist discusses
love, rage, and terror.

And the second violinist reports on the latest coup
in Afghanistan.

A gazelle leaps
in October light.

I am dazzled.

Magnetized

Jimson weed
has nothing to do
with the blueprint of a house,
or a white macaw.

But an iron bar,
magnetized, has a north and south
pole that attract.
Demagnetized, it has nothing
at either end.

The mind magnetizes
everything it touches.
A knife in a dog
has nothing to do
with the carburetor of an engine:

to all appearances,
to all appearances.

Knife at the Jugular

Sentenced to two consecutive
life terms, Robert Francis may be
paroled in twenty years. He may

walk out of jail at forty,
a free man. But the world travels
at the speed of light.

He will be a miner staggering
out of a collapsed mine. People
will have assumed he died

years ago. And, at forty,
the world will feel like *jamais*
vu. The barbed wire and

sunlight will be his only
friends. Perhaps, he will discern
freedom as a rat swimming in

a ditch, or pleasure as the
smell of green tea. And the full
moon, crazed with the voices

of dead men, will make him
relive again and again the double
ax murder. And will he know

himself? The Inuit have
thirty words describing varieties
of ice. I see a man in

twenty years walking into the
sunlight. He will know a thousand
words for varieties of pain.

His first act may be a knife
at the jugular, and his ensuing acts
may be terrors of the earth.

Pouilly-Fuissé

1

Foxes and pheasants adorn
the store window. A woman sells
dried anise, dried purple

mallow, and caviar inside.
But we don't live on purple mallow,
or Pouilly-Fuissé. I think

of the Africans I met
going to pick grapes at
$1.40 an hour.

2

A man trying to sell roses
throws water, and, instead of sprinkling,
drenches the roses. And

an old woman carrying leeks
wears shoes at least three sizes too large,
and walks almost crippled.

But, then, they make a world of
leeks and roses.

Alba

South light
wakes us. I turn
to your touch,
your long hair, and
slow kisses.
A wren sings in
the clear light.
Red cassia
blossoms in your
hands. And all
day the wren sings
in the day's
branches.

The Opal

Nailing up chicken wire on the frame house,
or using a chalk line, or checking a level at a glance
gets to be easy.
                    We install double-pane windows
pressurized with argon between the panes
for elevations over 4500'.
                                        And use pick and shovel
to dig for the footing for the annex. Lay cinder blocks,
and check levels. Pour the cement floor, and
use wood float and steel trowel to finish the surface
as it sets.
            Nailing into rough, dense, knotted
two-by-twelves, or using a chalk line to mark the locations
of the fire blocks, or checking the level of a
stained eight-by-ten window header gets to be
easier.
        In nailing up chicken wire, we learn
how to cut for the *canal,* pull the wire up over the
firewall, make cuts for the corners, tuck it
around back, and nail two-head nails into the stud.
And when the footing is slightly uneven and we are
laying a first row of cinder blocks, find that a
small pebble under a corner often levels the top
to the row.
              And, starting on rock lath, the various
stages of a house—cutting *vigas,* cleaning aspens for
latillas, installing oak doors, or plastering the
adobe wall—are facets of a cut opal.

Pentimento

In sepia, I draw a face and hands,
a river, a hawk. When I read your letter,
and feel the silences, the slow

changes in perspective, in feeling,
I make a fresco—fading even as it's painted.
It's pentimento: knowing the original

sepia lines, and the changes:
the left hand in darkness, a face, effaced,
in fading light, and the right hand

pointing to a Giotto-blue river, a blue hawk,
in a moment of grace.

The Weather Shifts

Unemployed, I recollect setting a plumb
line for the doorjambs to a house,
recollect nailing a rebar through two corbels
locked in a 60° angle into a post; and
smell unpicked cherries, fragrant,
in the dark rich earth. It is a pellucid
night in January: and the mind has its
own shifts in weather: a feel for light
from a star, or for a woman's voice,
a recognition of the world's greed,
of a death march on the Philippines, or
of being shot by an arrow dipped in curare.
Drinking tequila, I watch the moon
rise slowly over the black hills; a bird
sings, somewhere, out in the junipers.

*

Juniper Fires

Juniper
fires burn in the crisp night.
I am inebriated
on juniper smoke. And as my mind clears,
I see a white crane standing, one-legged, in the snow.
And see clearly the
rocks, and shaggy pines, the winter moon, and
creek.

Frost

Notice each windowpane has a different
swirling pattern of frost etched on the glass.

And notice how slowly the sun melts
the glaze. It is indelible: a fossil of a fern,

or a coelacanth, or a derelict who
rummages in his pockets and pulls out a few

apple cores. Notice the peculiar
angle of light in the slow shift of sunrise.

Where is the whir of the helicopter?
The search for escaped convicts in the city?

Be amazed at the shine and the wet.
Simply to live is a joy.

Black Lightning

A blind girl
stares at me,
then types out ten lines
in braille.

The air has a scent
of sandalwood and
arsenic; a night-blooming cereus
blooms on a dark path.

I look at the
short and long flow
of the lines:
and guess at garlic,
the sun, a silver desert rain,
and palms.

Or is it simply
about hands, a river of light,
the ear of a snail,
or rags?

And, stunned, I feel
the nerves of my hand flashing
in the dark, feel
the world as black
lightning.

Piranhas

piranhas
in a wine-dark river.
a radio station on antarctica sends messages
to outer space,
listens to quasars pulsing in the spiral nebula of andromeda.
a banker goes for a drive
in a red mercedes,
smokes black russian sobranie from england.
the sun
rides a red appaloosa to the gold mountains in the west;
then, incognito, shows up in questa:
wearing shades, carrying a geiger counter, and
prospecting for plutonium.
the history of the world
is in a museum in albania;
the price of admission is one dollar.
a kgb agent
has located trotsky's corpse,
and, under the guise of a gardener, enters his house
and breaks open his casket, and
shatters his cranium with an ice pick.
lepers
in a cathedral are staring up at the rose window.
o window of light:
we are falling
into a bottomless lake full of piranhas—
the piranhas, luminous, opalescent,
in the black water.
o paris, venice, moscow, buenos aires, saigon, kuala lumpur:
we are sailing up the wine-dark
river.

Impressions of the New Mexico Legislature

The lieutenant governor sits in the center
behind an oak desk. Below him, the reader of bills
reads at thirty miles per hour to pass or defeat
a bill depending on his cue.
                                        One senator
talks on the phone to Miss Española; another, a thug,
opens his briefcase, takes out a bottle
of whiskey, a shot glass, and begins drinking.
Bills from various committees are meanwhile passed
without comment. Finally, a bill is introduced,
and the lieutenant governor asks that the
content be explained.
                                A senator rises, speaks
into a microphone: "Bill 345-B is one of my most
important pieces of legislation. It commemorates
J.D. Arguello and H.R. Lucero who died last year
while firefighting. It also specifically commends
Victor de la Cruz who is now crippled."
                                                        Another
senator rises, introduces a bill to change the
composition of the podiatrists' board. Two members
of the public are to be on it. The lieutenant
governor asks what the requirements for the public
are. One senator quips, "Athlete's foot," is
out of order, and is silenced.
                                        The senators quickly
agree that one member of the public is sufficient.
The lieutenant governor says, "All those in favor
may say 'aye,' those opposed may raise their feet."

Cedar Fires

Cedar fires burn in my heart.
You speak of emeralds, cocaine, and henna.

You are slow rain fragrant in the eucalyptus,
in the silver leaves.

At night we look out at the Pleiades.
I think of the antelope carved in the rock

at Puyé: carved, perhaps, seven hundred
years ago. And, now, we touch the Pleiades.

For two weeks, seven hundred years,
cedar fires burn in my heart.

The Murmur

The doctor flicks on a light,
puts up the X-rays of our three-day-old child,
and diagnoses a shunt between
left and right ventricle,
claims an erratic electrocardiogram test
confirms his findings. Your child,
he says, may live three to six weeks unless
surgery is performed.

Two days later, a pediatric cardiologist
looks at the same X-rays and EKG test,
pronounces them normal,
and listens with disinterest to the murmur.
I think, then, of the birth:
mother and child in a cesarean,
the rush of blood in the umbilical cord
is a river pulsating with light.

And, as water rippling in a pond
ricochets off rocks, the network of
feelings between father and mother
and child is an ever-shifting web.
It is nothing on your doctor's X-ray
scanner; but, like minerals lit up
under a black light, it is an iridescent
red and green and indigo.

The Corona

Knife-edge
days and shimmering nights.
Our child watches the shifting sunlight and leaves.
The world shimmers, shimmers.

Smoke goes up the flue,
and spins, unravels in the wind.
Something in me unravels after long thought.
And my mind flares:
as if the sun and moon lock in an eclipse,
and the sun's corona flares out.

It is a fire
out of gasoline and rags
that makes us take nothing for granted.
And it is love, spontaneous,
flaring,
that makes us feel
like a cougar approaching a doe in labor,
makes us pause and move on.

Olive Night

The Jemez
Indians mention the Los Ojos bar.
I think of the Swiss
Army practicing maneuvers in the Alps.
The world is a hit-and-run, an armed robbery, and a fight.
I think of the evening star.
And ripen, as an olive ripens, in a cool
summer night.

*

The Cloud Chamber

A neighbor
rejects chemotherapy and the hospital;
and, instead, writes
a farewell letter to all her friends
before she dies.

I look at a wasp nest;
and, in the maze of hexagons,
find a few
white eggs, translucent, revealing formed wasps,
but wasps never to be born.

A pi-meson in a cloud chamber
exists for a thousandth of a second,
but the circular track
it leaves on a film
is immortal.

Empty Words

He describes eagle feathers with his hands.
He signs the rustle of pine needles on a mountain
path in sunlight, the taste of green water,
herding sheep in a canyon, the bones of a horse bleached
in sunlight, purple thistles growing in red dirt,
locoweed in bloom.

My mind is like a tumbleweed rolling
in the wind, smashing against the windshields of cars,
but rolling, rolling until nothing is left.
I sit in the sunlight, eyes closed:
empty mind, empty hands. I am a
great horned owl hunting in a night with no moon.

And this Indian, deaf-mute, is like a Serbian
in a twenty-four-hour truck stop,
is a yellow sandhill crane lost in Albuquerque.
I see the red blooms of a nasturtium battered
in a hailstorm. I see the bleached white bones of a horse
at the bottom of a canyon. And I see his hands,
empty hands, and words, empty words.

Tsankawi

The men hiked on a loop trail
past the humpbacked flute player and
a creation spiral petroglyph,
then up a ladder to the top of the mesa
and met the women there.

A flock of wild geese wheeled
in shifting formation over the mesa,
then flew south climbing higher and higher
and disappearing in clear sunlight.
The ceremony was simple: a blessing
of rings by "water which knows no
boundaries," and then a sprinkling of baskets
with blue cornmeal.

I write of this a week later
and think of Marie, who, at San Ildefonso,
opened the door to her house to us.
And we were deeply moved.
I hear these lines from the wedding:
"In our country, wind blows, willows live,
you live, I live, we live."

Antares

You point to
Antares.
The wind rustles the cottonwood leaves.
And the intermittent

rain sounds like a fifty-
string zither. A red lotus blossoms
in the air. And, touching you,
I am like light from

Antares. It has taken me light-
years to arrive.

The Owl

The path was purple in the dusk.
I saw an owl, perched,
on a branch.

And when the owl stirred, a fine dust
fell from its wings. I was
silent then. And felt

the owl quaver. And at dawn, waking,
the path was green in the
May light.

The Cornucopia

Grapes grow up a difficult and
sloped terrain. A soft line of poplars
shimmers in the disappearing light.
At midnight, the poor move
into the train stations of Italy,
spread out blankets for the children,
and pretend to the police they have tickets
and are waiting for a train.

The statue of Bacchus is a contrast
with his right hand holding a shallow but
wine-brimming cup. His left hand
reaches easily into the cornucopia
where grapes ripen and burst open.
It is a vivid dream: to wake
from the statue's grace and life force
to the suffering in the streets.

But the truth is the cornucopia
is open to all who are alive,
who look and feel the world in
its pristine beauty—as a dragonfly
hovering in the sunlight over clear
water; and who feel the world
as a luminous world—as green plankton
drifting at night in the sea.

The Chance

The blue-black mountains are etched
with ice. I drive south in fading light.
The lights of my car set out before
me, and disappear before my very eyes.
And as I approach thirty, the distances
are shorter than I guess? The mind
travels at the speed of light. But for
how many people are the passions
ironwood, ironwood that hardens and hardens?
Take the ex-musician, insurance salesman,
who sells himself a policy on his own life;
or the magician who has himself locked
in a chest and thrown into the sea,
only to discover he is caught in his own chains.
I want a passion that grows and grows.
To feel, think, act, and be defined
by your actions, thoughts, feelings.
As in the bones of a hand in an X-ray,
I want the clear white light to work
against the fuzzy blurred edges of the darkness:
even if the darkness precedes and follows
us, we have a chance, briefly, to shine.

The Network

In 1861, George Hew sailed in a rowboat
from the Pearl River, China, across
the Pacific Ocean to San Francisco.
He sailed alone. The photograph of him
in a museum disappeared. But, in the mind,
he is intense, vivid, alive. What is
this fact but another fact in a world
of facts, another truth in a vast network
of truths? It is a red maple leaf
flaming out at the end of its life,
revealing an incredibly rich and complex
network of branching veins. We live
in such a network: the world is opaque,
translucent, or, suddenly, lucid,
vibrant. The air is alive and hums
then. Speech is too slow to the mind.
And the mind's speech is so quick it breaks
the sound barrier and shatters glass.

Fauve

Caw Caw, Caw Caw Caw.
To comprehend a crow
you must have a crow's mind.
To be the night rain,
silver, on black leaves,
you must live in the
shine and wet. Some people
drift in their lives:
green-gold plankton,
phosphorescent, in the sea.
Others slash: a knife
at a yellow window shade
tears open the light.
But to live digging deep
is to feel the blood
in you rage as rivers,
is to feel love and hatred
as fibers of a rope,
is to catch the scent
of a wolf, and turn wild.

Fern, Coal, Diamond

The intense pressure of the earth
makes coal out of ferns, diamonds out of coal.
The intense pressure of the earth
is within us, and makes coal
and diamond desires.

For instance, we are a river
flowing and flowing out to sea,
an oak fire flaring and flaring in a night
with no wind, or, protean,
a river, a fire, an oak, a hawk, a wind.

And at first light,
I mark the stages of our growth:
mark fern, coal, diamond,
mark a pressure transforming
even broken nails and broken glass into
clear molten light.

The Axis

I hear on the radio that Anastasio Somoza
has fled Managua, is already in Florida,

and about to disappear on a world cruise.
Investigators in this country are meanwhile

analyzing the volcanic eruptions on Io,
or are studying the erratic respiratory

pattern of a sea horse to find the origin
of life. The fact is, we know so little,

but are so quick to interpret, to fit facts
to our schemata. For instance, the final

collapse of the Nicaraguan dictatorship
makes me wonder if the process of change

is a dialectic. Or is our belief in a
pattern what sustains it? Is the recent

history a clear pattern: a dictatorship
followed by a popular revolt, followed by

a renewed dictatorship exercising greater
repression, ended by a violent revolution?

I want to speak of opposites that depend
on and define each other: as in a

conversation, you feel silence in speech,
or speech in silence. Or, as in a

counterpoint when two melodies overlap and
resonate, you feel the sea in the desert,

or feel that the body and mind are
inseparable. Then you wonder if day and

night are indeed opposites. You knock the
gyroscope off the axis of its spinning,

so that one orientation in the world vanishes,
and the others appear infinite.

River River

1987

The Leaves of a Dream Are the Leaves of an Onion

1

Red oak leaves rustle in the wind.
Inside a dream, you dream the leaves
scattered on dirt, and feel it
as an instance of the chance configuration

to your life. All night you feel
red horses galloping in your blood,
hear a piercing siren, and are in love
with the inexplicable. You walk

to your car, find the hazard lights
blinking: find a rust-brown knife, a trout,
a smashed violin in your hands.
And then you wake, inside the dream,

to find tangerines ripening in the silence.
You peel the leaves of the dream
as you would peel the leaves off an onion.
The layers of the dream have no core,

no essence. You find a tattoo of
a red scorpion on your body.
You simply laugh, shiver in the frost,
and step back into the world.

2

A Galápagos turtle has nothing to do
with the world of the neutrino.
The ecology of the Galápagos Islands
has nothing to do with a pair of scissors.
The cactus by the window has nothing to do
with the invention of the wheel.
The invention of the telescope
has nothing to do with a red jaguar.
No. The invention of the scissors
has everything to do with the invention of the telescope.
A map of the world has everything to do
with the cactus by the window.
The world of the quark has everything to do
with a jaguar circling in the night.
The man who sacrifices himself and throws a Molotov
cocktail at a tank has everything to do
with a sunflower that bends to the light.

3

Open a window and touch the sun,
or feel the wet maple leaves flicker in the rain.
Watch a blue crab scuttle in clear water,
or find a starfish in the dirt.
Describe the color green to the colorblind,
or build a house out of pain.

The world is more than you surmise.
Take the pines, green-black, slashed by light,
etched by wind, on the island
across the riptide body of water.
Describe the thousand iridescent needles
to a blind albino Tarahumara.

In a bubble chamber, in a magnetic field,
an electron spirals and spirals in to the center,
but the world is more than such a dance:
a spiraling in to the point of origin,
a spiraling out in the form of a
wet leaf, a blue crab, or a green house.

4

The heat ripples ripple the cactus.
Crushed green glass in a parking lot
or a pile of rhinoceros bones
gives off heat, though you might not notice it.

The heat of a star can be measured
under a spectrometer, but not
the heat of the mind, or the heat of Angkor Wat.
And the rubble of Angkor Wat

gives off heat; so do apricot blossoms
in the night, green fish, black bamboo,
or a fisherman fishing in the snow.
And an angstrom of shift turns the pleasure

into pain. The ice that rips the fingerprint
off your hand gives off heat;
and so does each moment of existence.
A red red leaf, disintegrating in the dirt,

burns with the heat of an acetylene flame.
And the heat rippling off
the tin roof of the adobe house
is simply the heat you see.

5

What is the secret to a Guarneri violin?
Wool dipped in an indigo bath turns bluer
when it oxidizes in the air. Marat is
changed in the minds of the living.
A shot of tequila is related to Antarctica
shrinking. A crow in a bar or red snapper on ice
is related to the twelve-tone method
of composition. And what does the tuning of timpani
have to do with the smell of your hair?
To feel, at thirty, you have come this far—
to see a bell over a door as a bell
over a door, to feel the care and precision
of this violin is no mistake, nor is the
sincerity and shudder of passion by which you live.

6

Crush an apple, crush a possibility.
No single method can describe the world;
therein is the pleasure
of chaos, of leaps in the mind.
A man slumped over a desk in an attorney's office
is a parrotfish caught in a seaweed mass.
A man who turns to the conversation in a bar
is a bluefish hooked on a cigarette.
Is the desire and collapse of desire in an unemployed carpenter
the instinct of salmon to leap upstream?
The smell of eucalyptus can be incorporated
into a theory of aggression.
The pattern of interference in a hologram
replicates the apple, knife, horsetails on the table,
but misses the sense of chaos, distorts
in its singular view. Then
touch, shine, dance, sing, be, becoming, be.

The Aphrodisiac

"Power is my aphrodisiac."
Power enables him to
connect a candlelit dinner
to the landing on the moon.
He sees a plot in the acid
content of American soil,
malice in the configuration
of palm-leaf shadows.
He is obsessed with
the appearance of democracy
in a terrorized nation.
If the price of oil
is an owl claw, a nuclear
reactor is a rattlesnake
fang. He has no use
for the song of an oriole,
bright yellow wings.
He refuses to consider
a woman in a wheelchair
touching the shadow of
a sparrow, a campesino
dreaming of spring.
He revels in the instant
before a grenade explodes.

The Ansel Adams Card

You left a trail of bad checks in forty-six states.
When you were finally arrested on a check for $36.10,
you no longer knew how many aliases you had burned
out. You simply knew you had waited too long at the checkout
counter. The police found five sets of current driver's
licenses in your car, titles to ten other cars,
two diamond rings, and $2500 cash.

You started by running off with an ex-convict,
forging your mother's signature at the post office,
collecting her mail, and cashing a check.
You bought a car and groceries with the check:
took off, then, to Chicago. The scenario
was to open a checking account for fifty dollars,
withdraw forty at the end of the day, and use the blank
checks to shop with. Again and again: how many
times until you saw your signature at the checkout counter?
Once, you thought quickly, pulled out a license
with a different name, ran out to your husband
waiting in the car.

And he was scot-free: a tattoo of white lightning
on his arms. Now he is a used-car salesman in Kansas City—
forging car titles and duplicating sales?
I see you as a green leaf in sunshine
after a rain. If you are paroled in July,
what will happen? Surely you won't forget life in prison,
jumping bail, on the run, the rape, the humiliation,
the arrest? But you are walking on glass.
You are now married to an inmate in Texarkana.
I give you this Ansel Adams card with one aspen, leafy,
against a forest, one aspen bright in the sun.

New Wave

He listens to a punk rock group,
Dead on Arrival,
on his miniature Sony headphones and cassette recorder.
With the volume turned up,
the noise of the world
can't touch him.
No one's going to tell *him* what to do:
whether to drive
his car up an arroyo,
or wire the house with explosives.
He's given us the rap
on New Wave:
how it's noise and is disgusting—
though we suspect
whatever he dislikes is New Wave.
His mind is a Geiger counter bombarded with radiation:
the clusters of
click click click click, click click
a daily dose of carcinogens
without which
it would be impossible to live.
He watches us listen to a Jewish astrologer
reading a horoscope,
and glances out the window.
Now he flips
the cassette and turns up the volume.
I can see the headlines now:
Juvenile Detonates House,
pleads temporary insanity
due to the effects of listening to Agent Orange.

Every Where and Every When

1

Catch a moth in the Amazon; pin it under glass.
See the green-swirling magenta-flecked wings

miming a fierce face. And dead—watch it fly.
Throw a piece of juniper into a fire.

Search out the Odeon in Zurich to find Lenin or Klee.
No one has a doctrine of recollection to

bring back knowledge of what was, is?
The Odeon café is not the place to look

for Lenin's fingerprint. The piece of burning juniper
has the sound of the bones of your hands

breaking. And the moth at the window, magenta-flecked,
green-swirling, is every where and every when.

2

Everything is supposed to fit: mortise and tenon,
arteries and veins, hammer, anvil, stirrup in the ear,

but it does not fit. Someone was executed
today. Tomorrow friends of the executed will execute

the executers. And this despair is the intensifying
fever and chill, in shortening intervals,

of a malaria patient. Evil is not a variety of
potato found in the Andes. The smell of a gardenia

is not scissors and sponge in the hands of
an inept surgeon. Everything is supposed to fit:

but wander through Cuzco and the orientation of
streets and plazas is too Spanish. Throw

hibiscus on a corpse. Take an aerial view;
see the city built in the shape of a jaguar's head.

3

I pick a few mushrooms in the hills,
but do not know the lethal from the edible.

I cannot distinguish red wood dyed
with cochineal or lac, but know that

cochineal with alum, tin, salt, and lime juice
makes a rosé, a red, a burgundy.

Is it true an antimatter particle
never travels as slowly as the speed of light,

and, colliding with matter, explodes?
The mind shifts as the world shifts.

I look out the window, watch Antares glow.
The world shifts as the mind shifts;

or this belief, at least, increases
the pleasure of it all—the smell of espresso

in the street, picking blueberries,
white-glazed, blue-black,

sieved gold from a river, this moment
when we spin and shine.

The Rehearsal

Xylophone, triangle, marimba, soprano, violin—
the musicians use stopwatches, map out
in sound the convergence of three rivers at a farm,

but it sounds like the jungle at midnight.
Caught in a blizzard and surrounded by wolves
circling closer and closer, you might

remember the smell of huisache on a warm spring night.
You might remember three deer startled and stopped
at the edge of a road in a black canyon.

A child wants to act crazy, acts crazy,
is thereby sane. If you ache with longing
or are terrified: ache, be terrified, be hysterical,

walk into a redwood forest and listen:
hear a pine cone drop into a pool of water.
And what is your life then? In the time

it takes to make a fist or open your hand,
the musicians have stopped. But a life only stops
when what you want is no longer possible.

Kayaking at Night on Tomales Bay

Kayak on the black water,
and feel a gold feather float in the air.
Pick up a red shard in the dirt,
and feel someone light a
candle and sing.

A man may die crashing into a redwood house,
or die as someone pries
open an oyster.
A kayaker may hit a rock, and
drown at the bottom of a waterfall.

Is the world of the dead
a world of memory? Or a world of ten dimensions?
Calculate the number of
configurations to a tangram?
Compute the digits of pi?

Kayak on the black water,
and feel the moonlight glisten the pines.
Drift, drift, and drifting:
the lights of cars on the road take a
thousand years to arrive.

Mistaking Water Hemlock for Parsley

Mistaking water hemlock for parsley,
I die two hours
later in the hospital;
or I turn the shish kebab on the hibachi,
and reel, crash
to the floor, die of a ruptured aorta.

Then you place an ear of blue corn
in my left hand,
tie a single turkey feather
around my right ankle.
I hear the coffin nailed shut,
hear green singing finches in the silence.

And in the silence I float on water,
feel an equilibrium,
feel the gravitational pull of the universe
slow everything down
and begin to draw everything back
to the center.

Then a star is a taste of olives,
a sun the shine on the black wings of ravens.
I wake, and joy and love, and feel
each passion makes me
protean, wiser, stronger.
I want to live and live and live and live.

Evil Grigri

Evil grigri:
taste acid in the word *sybaritic.*
Feel deer antlers polished in rain and sun;
taste green almonds,
the polar icecap of Mars melting at the tip of your tongue.

Is it possible to wake
dressed in a tuxedo smoking a cigarette staring at a firing squad?
A man is cursed
when he remembers he cannot remember his dream;
taste sugar in the word *voluptuous;*
feel a macaw feather brush across your closed eyelids.

See the dead laugh at the pile of shoes at Dachau.
See as a man with one eye
the dead alive and singing,
walking down the equinoctial axis of the midnight street.

Now feel how the ocarina of your body
waits for pleasure to blow and make an emerald sound in the air;
make an apotropaic prayer
that the day's evil become the day's wild thyme:

say guava-passionflower-hibiscus salt,
say sun-sea wave,
say wind-star, venom-night,
say mango-river, eucalyptus-scented fang.

The Pulse

A woman in a psychiatric ward
is hysterical; she has to get a letter
to God by tomorrow or

the world will end. Which root
of a chiasma grows and grows?
Which dies? An analysis of

the visual cortex of the brain
confines your worldview even as you
try to enlarge it? I walk

down an arroyo lined with old tires
and broken glass, feel a pulse,
a rhythm in silence, a slow

blooming of leaves. I know
it is unlikely, but feel I could
find the bones of a whale

as easily as a tire iron.
I shut my eyes, green water flowing
in the acequia never returns.

The Diamond Point

Use the diamond point of grief:
incise a clear hibiscus in the windowpane.
A child picks apples in autumn light;
five minutes resemble a day?
But an aquamarine instant dropped
into water makes an entire pool shine.
Do you feel the forsythia about to explode?
The flow in a dead seal washed to shore?
I see the sloping street
to your house, bird-of-paradise in bloom:

silence when you lift the receiver off the phone,
shaft of spring light when you say, "Hello."
I see you smile in a flower dress—
intense pain, intense joy—waving goodbye,
goodbye, goodbye, goodbye, goodbye
1947, 1960, 1967, 1972, 1981.
A firework explodes in a purple chrysanthemum:
ooh and aah and then, then
use the diamond point of grief:
incise a clear hibiscus in the windowpane.

Metastasis

Noon summer solstice light shines on a creation spiral petroglyph.
We stare up at a pictograph of a left hand,
a new moon, a supernova of 1054.
I dream of touching a rattlesnake,
want to find a fossil
of a green ginkgo leaf here in Chaco Wash.
I have not forgotten the death of Josephine Miles,
but forget grief,
that fried tripe;
I want to hike the thousand summer trails,
become sun, moon.
A rattlesnake slides into a coil:
if grief, grief, if pain, pain, if joy, joy.
In a night rain
all the emotions of a day become pure and shining.
I think, I no longer think:
metastasis: noon summer solstice light: turpentine, rags:
the new leaves of a peach delicate
and of light-green hue.

Horse Face

A man in prison is called horse face, but does nothing
when everyone in the tailor shop has sharp cold scissors;

he remembers the insult but laughs it off. Even as he
laughs, a Cattaraugus Indian welding a steel girder

turns at a yell which coincides with the laugh and slips
to his death. I open a beer, a car approaches a garage.

The door opens, a light comes on, inside rakes gleam;
a child with dysentery washes his hands in cow piss.

I find a trail of sawdust, walk in a dead killer's
hardened old shoes, and feel how difficult it is to

sense the entire danger of a moment: a horse gives birth
to a foal, power goes out in the city, a dancer

stops in the dark and listening for the noise that was scored
in the performance hears only sudden panicked yells.

The Negative

A man hauling coal in the street is stilled forever.
Inside a temple, instead of light

a slow shutter lets the darkness in.
I see a rat turn a corner running from a man with a chair trying to smash it,

see people sleeping at midnight in a Wuhan street on bamboo beds,
a dead pig floating, bloated, on water.

I see a photograph of a son smiling who two years ago fell off a cliff
and his photograph is in each room of the apartment.

I meet a woman who had smallpox as a child, was abandoned by her mother
but who lived, now has two daughters, a son, a son-in-law;

they live in three rooms and watch a color television.
I see a man in blue work clothes whose father was a peasant

who joined the Communist party early but by the time of the Cultural Revolution
had risen in rank and become a target of the Red Guards.

I see a woman who tried to kill herself with an acupuncture needle
but instead hit a vital point and cured her chronic asthma.

A Chinese poet argues that the fundamental difference between East and West
is that in the East an individual does not believe himself

in control of his fate but yields to it.
As a negative reverses light and dark

these words are prose accounts of personal tragedy becoming metaphor,
an emulsion of silver salts sensitive to light,

laughter in the underground bomb shelter converted into a movie theater,
lovers in the Summer Palace park.

Wasabi

Quinine is to cinchona
as pain is to nerves? No,
as the depletion of ozone is to a city? No,

like a DNA double helix,
the purity of intention
is linked to the botched attempt.

The zing of a circular saw
is linked in time to
the smell of splintery charred plywood dust.

And the scent of red ginger
to a field guide is as
a blueprint to walking out of sunlight

into a cool stone Lama temple?
The mind at chess,
the mind at go: here

the purpose is not to prevail,
but to taste—as ikebana
is to spring cherry blossoms—wasabi.

The Solderer

I watch a man soldering positive and negative speaker
wires to a plug inhale tin-lead alloy smoke.

He does not worry about a shift in the solar wind.
He does not worry about carcinogens.

Are his mind and memory as precise as his hands?
To suffer and suffer is not a necessary and sufficient

condition for revelation; open up a box of
Balinese flowers, roots, bark: the history of civilization

is to know you do not know what to do.
In my mind I practice rubbing a bronze spouting bowl

with both hands. The bowl begins to hum
and a standing wave makes the water splash up into my face.

I am stunned to hear a man who wore a T-shirt
with a silk-screened tie shot himself and is in critical

condition in the hospital. No one wants to
die suspended in air like gold dust flecked by sunlight.

Renga

We hunger for the iridescent shine of an abalone shell

Stare at a newspaper, see the latest terrors

Want the sound of hail on a tin roof to reverberate forever

Want to feel the echo as we wash a rag, pick broccoli, sneeze

The sound does not make us forget the terrors

But the terrors are lived then as water in a stream

We hold, as in a tea ceremony, a bowl with both hands

Turn it a quarter-turn, and another, and another

And when we see the green stillness

See the abalone shine, abalone shine

Ten Thousand to One

The Phoenicians guarded a recipe that required
ten thousand murex shells to make
an ounce of Tyrian purple.

Scan the surface of Aldebaran with a radio wave;
grind lapis lazuli
into ultramarine.

Search the summer sky for an Anasazi turkey constellation;
see algae under an electron microscope
resemble a Magellanic Cloud.

A chemist tried to convert benzene into quinine,
but blundered into a violet
aniline dye instead.

Have you ever seen maggots feed on a dead rat?
Listen to a red-tailed hawk glide
over the hushed spruce and

pines in a canyon. Feel a drop of water roll
down a pine needle, and glisten,
hanging, at the tip.

To a Composer

Red chair, blue chair, white chair, big chair, chair.
No, this is not the taste
of unripe persimmons,
nor standing on a New York street in December inhaling shish kebab smoke.
The dissonant sounds played on a piano
become macaws perched on cages.
A green Amazon parrot with yellow-tipped wings
lands on your shoulder.
The background hum
of loudspeakers becomes a humid environment.
You may open this door and walk into the aviary
when you least expect to,
startled walk on redwood planks over huge-leafed tropical plants
as a red-billed toucan flaps by.
Dirty utensils are piled in the sink,
coffee grounds clog the drain.
So what if the plumber pouring sulfuric acid
gives you a look
when you open the refrigerator
and pull out a just solidified chocolate turkey in a pan?
This is not 5:14 sharpening a pencil
but inhaling deeply and feeling the stream of air poured out through a *shakuhachi*
become a style of living.

Shooting Star

1

In a concussion,
the mind severs the pain:
you don't remember flying off a motorcycle,
and landing face-first
in a cholla.

But a woman stabbed in her apartment,
by a prowler searching for
money and drugs,
will never forget her startled shriek
die in her throat,
blood soaking into the floor.

The quotidian violence of the world
is like a full moon rising over the Ortiz Mountains;
its pull is everywhere.
But let me live a life of violent surprise
and startled joy. I want to
thrust a purple iris into your hand,
give you a sudden embrace.

I want to live as Wang Hsi-chih lived
writing characters in gold ink on black silk—
not to frame on a wall,
but to live the splendor now.

2

Deprived of sleep, she hallucinated
and, believing she had sold the genetic
research on carp, signed a confession.
Picking psilocybin mushrooms in the mountains

of Veracruz, I hear tin cowbells
in the slow rain, see men wasted on pulque
sitting under palm trees. Is it
so hard to see things as they truly are:

a route marked in red ink on a map,
the shadows of apricot leaves thrown
in wind and sun on a wall? It is
easy to imagine a desert full of agaves

and golden barrel cactus, red earth, a red sun.
But to truly live one must see things
as they are, as they might become:
a wrench is not a fingerprint

on a stolen car, nor baling wire
the undertow of the ocean. I may hallucinate,
but see the men in drenched clothes
as men who saw and saw and refuse to see.

3

Think of being a judge or architect
or trombonist, and do not worry whether
thinking so makes it so. I overhear
two men talking in another room;

I cannot transcribe the conversation
word for word, but know if they are
vexed or depressed, joyful or nostalgic.
An elm leaf floats on a pond.

Look, a child wants to be a cardiologist
then a cartographer, but wanting so
does not make it so. It is not
a question of copying out the Heart Sutra

in your own blood on an alabaster wall.
It is not a question of grief or joy.
But as a fetus grows and grows,
as the autumn moon ripens the grapes,

greed and cruelty and hunger for power
ripen us, enable us to grieve, act,
laugh, shriek, see, see it all as
the water on which the elm leaf floats.

4

Write out the memories of your life
in red-gold disappearing ink, so that it all
dies, no lives. Each word you speak
dies, no lives. Is it all
at once in the mind? I once stepped
on a sea urchin, used a needle to dig out
the purple spines; blood soaked my hands.
But one spine was left, and I carried
it a thousand miles. I saw then
the olive leaves die on the branch,
saw dogs tear flesh off a sheep's corpse.
To live at all is to grieve;
but, once, to have it all at once
is to see a shooting star: shooting star
shooting star.

The Silence

We walk through a yellow-ochre adobe house:
the windows are smeared with grease,
the doors are missing. Rain leaks
through the ceilings of all the rooms,
and the ribs of saguaro thrown across *vigas*
are dark, wet, and smell. The view outside
of red-faded and turquoise-faded adobes
could be Chihuahua, but it isn't.
I stop and look through an open doorway,
see wet newspapers are rotting in mud
in the small center patio.
I suddenly see red bougainvillea blooming
against a fresh whitewashed wall,
smell yellow wisteria through an open
window on a warm summer night;
but, no, a shot of cortisone is no cure
for a detaching retina. I might just
as well see a smashed dog in the street,
a boojum tree pushing its way up
through asphalt. And as we turn
and arrive where we began, I note
the construction of the house is
simply room after room forming a square.
We step outside, and the silence is as
water is, taking the shape of the container.

Keokea

Black wattles along the edge of the clearing
below the house: a few koa plants are fenced in.

An old horse nibbles grass near the loquat tree.
Sunburned from hiking twelve miles into a volcano,

I do not know what I am looking at. Koa?
I want to walk into an empty charred house

and taste a jacaranda blossom.
Here Sun Yat-sen pounded his fist, sold opium,

dreamed the Chinese Revolution until blood broke
inside his brain? Marvin Miura is running

for political office; he wants aquaculture
for Maui, a ti leaf wrapped around a black river

stone, and he may get it. But one needs
to walk into a charred house where the sensuous

images of the world can be transformed. Otherwise
we can sit up all night on the redwood decking,

argue greed and corruption, the price of sugarcane,
how many pearls Imelda Marcos owns.

Early Autumn

I almost squashed a tarantula on the road.
And once when I found
earthstars growing under pines

almost sliced one open
but stopped.
The Mayans keyed their lives to the motion of Venus

but timing is human not Hegelian.
A revolutionary never waits
for cities to arrive

at appropriate orthodox Marxist conditions
to act.
A man used a chain saw

to cut yellow cedar,
but when he finished
discovered a minus tide had beached his skiff.

I've lived 12,680 days
and dreamed gold plankton flashing in my hands.
It flashes now

as I watch
red dragonflies vanish over water.
A blue tarantula crossed Highway 285.

Nothing Can Heal the Severed Nerves of a Hand?

Nothing can heal the severed nerves of a hand?
No one can stop feeling the touch of things
as the nerves die? A wasp lands on a yellow
but still green-veined leaf floating on water—
two dead flies drift aside. An old man
draws a llama on roller skates, remembers
arguing cases in court, now argues in a wheelchair
with whoever arrives. The nurses hate him,
but forget a life lived without mallet and chisel
is lived without scars. Then think how long
it takes the body to heal, the mind to shine.
An acupuncturist pushes a needle into your ear:
you incandesce. Yes. Yes, more, all, no, less, none.
Prune the branches of a pear at midnight;
taste a pine needle on a branch without touching it;
feel a seed germinate in the dark, sending
down roots, sending up leaves, ah!

Splash, Flow

The unerring tragedy of our lives is to sail
a papyrus sailboat across the Atlantic Ocean,

discover corn fossils in China: splash, flow.
When the bones of a platypus are found at Third Mesa,

the *Koyemsi* will laugh. Watch a papyrus sailboat
slowly sink into the Mediterranean;

feel how grief, like a mordant, quietly attaches
pain to your nerves. *Now* splash, flow:

taste the sunrise shining inside your hands,
be jalapeño, wine, salt, gold, fire;

rejoice as your child finds a Malodorous Lepiota
under myrtle, smell the sea at night

as you hold the woman you love in your arms.

The Moment of Creation

A painter indicates the time of day
in a still life: afternoon light slants on a knife,
lemons, green wine bottle with some red wine.
We always leave something unfinished?
We want x and having x want y and having y want z?
I try to sense the moment of creation
in the shine on a sliced lemon. I want to
connect throwing gravel on mud to being hungry.
"Eat," a man from Afghanistan said
and pointed to old rotting apples in the opened car trunk.
I see a line of men dancing a cloud dance;
two women dance intricate lightning steps
at either end. My mistakes and failures
pulse in me even as moments of joy,
but I want the bright moments to resonate out
like a gamelan gong. I want to make
the intricate tessellated moments of our lives
a floor of jade, obsidian, turquoise, ebony, lapis.

Forget Fez

Algol, Mizar:
I wanted to become pure like the Arabic
names of stars,

but perhaps I have erred.
At sunrise

the song of an ordinary robin startles me.
I want to say vireo,

but it *is* a robin.
In bed I turn and breathe
with your breath,

remember four days ago opening my hands
to a man who blessed me

and others with an eagle feather.
Betelgeuse, Deneb:

moonshine on a clear summer night,
but the splendor
is to taste smoke in your hair.

Forget Fez.

Shuttle

She is making stuffing for the turkey;
a few pistachio shells are on the kitchen table.
He looks out the window at the thermometer,

but sees a winter melon with a white glaze
in a New York Chinatown store at night.
Large sea bass swim in a tank by the window;

there are delicate blue crabs in a can
climbing and climbing on each other to get out.
She is thinking of a tapestry of red horses

running across a Southwestern landscape
with blue mesas in the distance. A shuttle goes
back and forth, back and forth through

the different sheds. He is talking to a man
who photographs empty parks in New York,
sees the branches of a black magnolia in early December.

She is washing out yarn so it will pack
and cover the warp; perhaps the tension
isn't right; the texture of Churro fleece

makes her hands tingle; a pot of walnuts
boils on the stove. He turns on the radio,
and listening to Nigerian music

feels the rumble of a subway under the floor,
feels the warmth of his hands
as he watches the snow fall and fall.

Throwing Salt on a Path

I watch you throw salt on the path,
and see abalone divers point to the sun,
discuss the waves, then throw their

gear back into the car. I watch you
collect large flakes of salt off rocks,
smell sliced ginger and fresh red

shrimp smoking over a fire. Ah,
the light of a star never stops, but travels
at the expanding edge of the universe.

A Swiss gold watch ticks and ticks;
but when you cannot hear it tick anymore,
it turns transparent in your hand.

You see the clear gold wheels
with sharp minute teeth catching each
other and making each spin.

The salt now clears a path in the snow,
expands the edges of the universe.

Edna Bay

One day the men pulled a house off float logs
up on land with a five-ton winch and a system of pulleys,
while a woman with a broken tooth chewed aspirin

and watched. A man was cutting down a red cedar
with a chain saw when it kicked back in his face,
cut his chin and hand to bone. A neighbor called Ketchikan

through a marine operator and chartered a plane
out before dark. Life on Kosciusko Island
is run by the weather and tides. Is the rain today

from the southeast or southwest? If southeast,
the men go into the rain forest cursing:
it will be hard to dig out pilings for a house.

I see how these fishermen hate seiners and humpies,
want to spend days and days trolling at twenty-four fathoms.
I watch a great blue heron knife herring at low tide,

see a bald eagle circle and circle the shoreline.
One night with the full moon and a wind
on my face, I went across the bay in a skiff

looking at the rippling black water.
Days I will wake startled dreaming of bear,
see sheets of thin ice floating out in the bay.

Black Java Pepper

Despair, anger, grief:
as a seiner indiscriminately hauls
humpies, jellyfish, kelp,
we must—farouche,

recalcitrant—conversely
angle for sockeye.
Our civilization has no genetic code
to make wasps return

each spring to build a nest
by the water heater
in the shed. We must—igneous,
metamorphic—despite

such plans as to push Mt. Fuji into the ocean
to provide more land—
grind cracked black
Java pepper into our speech

so that—limestone into marble,
granite into gneiss—
we become through our griefs—
rain forest islands—song.

The Halibut

Dipping spruce branches into the calm water
to collect herring eggs
is an azure unthinking moment.
A fisherman never forgets the violet hue of December stars.
Does time make memory or memory make time polychromatic?
Squawk.
In a split second one hears a Steller's jay, raven,
car tires on gravel, chain saw, fly, wind chime.
This constellation of polychromatic sounds
becomes a crimson moment
that, fugitive-colored, will fade.
But one never forgets lighting kerosene lamps before noon.
In July when one has twenty hours of light
each second is fuchsia dyed.
One might be pouring Clorox down a hose to flush out an octopus
when one feels the moment explode,
when a fisherman using power crank and long line
looks into the water and sees
rising a two-hundred-pound halibut with bulging eyes.

Standing on an Alder Bridge over a Creek

At low tide, midnight, with a flashlight,
we walk along the shore stumbling
on rocks, slightly drunk, step

through a creek where arctic water pours in
over my boots; nothing to do but
go on. We come to a tidal pool,

stop, see the exposed colonies of blue-black
mussels, go up to a trail, come
to an alder bridge; stop:

let the mature mind consider danger,
guess the architecture of a Persian house
in a dream contains the sockeye

an osprey hungers for. If so,
then emerald *if*: no, despair?
Like the camouflage of snowy plover eggs

in sand and bright sunshine,
we stand on an alder bridge over a creek,
are the April starlight and laugh.

Here

Here a snail on a wet leaf shivers and dreams of spring.
Here a green iris in December.
Here the topaz light of the sky.
Here one stops hearing a twig break and listens for deer.
Here the art of the ventriloquist.
Here the obsession of a kleptomaniac to steal red pushpins.
Here the art of the alibi.
Here one walks into an abandoned farmhouse and hears a tarantella.
Here one dreamed a bear claw and died.
Here a humpback whale leaped out of the ocean.
Here the outboard motor stopped but a man made it to this island with one oar.
Here the actor forgot his lines and wept.
Here the art of prayer.
Here marbles, buttons, thimbles, dice, pins, stamps, beads.
Here one becomes terrified.
Here one wants to see as a god sees and becomes clear amber.
Here one is clear pine.

Parallax

"Kwakwha."
"Askwali."
The shift in Hopi when a man or woman says "thank you"
becomes a form of parallax.
A man travels

from Mindanao to Kyushu and says his inner geography
is enlarged by each new place.
Is it?
Might he not grow more by staring for twenty-four hours
at a single pine needle?

I watch a woman tip an ashtray and empty
a few ashes into her mouth,
but ah, I want
other soliloquies.
I want equivalents to Chu-ko Liang sending his fire ships

downstream into Ts'ao Ts'ao's fleet.
It does not mean
a geneticist must quit
and devote his life to the preservation of rhinoceros,
but it might mean

watching a thousand snow geese drift on water
as the sky darkens minute by minute.
"Kwakwha,"
"Askwali,"
whenever, wherever.

The Day Can Become a Zen Garden of Raked Sand

The day can become a Zen garden of raked sand
or a yellow tanager singing on a branch;

feel the terrors and pleasures of the morning:
in Tianjin all the foreigners are sent to a movie

and they must guess at what the authorities
do not wish them to see; dream a rainy landscape:

the Jemez Mountains breaking up in mist and jagged light
into a series of smaller but dazzling ranges;

to distinguish the smell of calendula from delphinium
is of no apparent consequence, but guess that

crucial moments in history involve an unobtrusive
point flaring into a startling revelation;

now be alive to the flowering chives by the window;
feel the potato plant in the whiskey barrel soak up sun;

feel this riparian light,
this flow where no word no water is.

The Unnameable River

1

Is it in the anthracite face of a coal miner,
crystallized in the veins and lungs of a steel
worker, pulverized in the grimy hands of a railroad engineer?
Is it in a child naming a star, coconuts washing
ashore, dormant in a volcano along the Rio Grande?

You can travel the four thousand miles of the Nile
to its source and never find it.
You can climb the five highest peaks of the Himalayas
and never recognize it.
You can gaze through the largest telescope
and never see it.

But it's in the capillaries of your lungs.
It's in the space as you slice open a lemon.
It's in a corpse burning on the Ganges,
in rain splashing on banana leaves.

Perhaps you have to know you are about to die
to hunger for it. Perhaps you have to go
alone into the jungle armed with a spear
to truly see it. Perhaps you have to
have pneumonia to sense its crush.

But it's also in the scissor hands of a clock.
It's in the precessing motion of a top
when a torque makes the axis of rotation describe a cone:
and the cone spinning on a point gathers
past, present, future.

2

In a crude theory of perception, the apple you
see is supposed to be a copy of the actual apple,
but who can step out of his body to compare the two?
Who can step out of his life and feel
the Milky Way flow out of his hands?

An unpicked apple dies on a branch;
that is all we know of it.
It turns black and hard, a corpse on the Ganges.
Then go ahead and map out three thousand miles of the Yangtze;
walk each inch, feel its surge and
flow as you feel the surge and flow in your own body.

And the spinning cone of a precessing top
is a form of existence that gathers and spins death and life into one.
It is in the duration of words, but beyond words—
river river river, river river.
The coal miner may not know he has it.
The steel worker may not know he has it.
The railroad engineer may not know he has it.
But it is there. It is in the smell
of an avocado blossom, and in the true passion of a kiss.

Archipelago

1995

Streamers

1

As an archaeologist unearths a mask with opercular teeth
and abalone eyes, someone throws a broken fan and extension cords
into a dumpster. A point of coincidence exists in the mind

resembling the tension between a denotation and its stretch
of definition: aurora: a luminous phenomenon consisting
of streamers or arches of light appearing in the upper atmosphere

of a planet's polar regions, caused by the emission of light
from atoms excited by electrons accelerated along the planet's
magnetic field lines. The mind's magnetic field lines.

When the red shimmering in the huge dome of sky stops,
a violet flare is already arcing up and across, while a man
foraging a dumpster in Cleveland finds some celery and charred fat.

Hunger, angst: the blue shimmer of emotion, water speeding
through a canyon; to see only to know: to wake finding
a lug nut, ticket stub, string, personal card, ink smear, $2.76.

2

A Kwakiutl wooden dish with a double-headed wolf
is missing from a museum collection. And as

the director checks to see if it was deaccessioned,
a man sitting on a stool under bright lights

shouts: a pachinko ball dropped vertiginously
but struck a chiming ring and ricocheted to the left.

We had no sense that a peony was opening,
that a thousand white buds of a Kyoto camellia

had opened at dusk and had closed at dawn.
When the man steps out of the pachinko parlor,

he will find himself vertiginously dropping
in starless space. When he discovers

that his daughter was cooking over smoking oil
and shrieked in a fatal asthma attack,

he will walk the bright streets in an implosion of grief,
his mind will become an imploding star,

he will know he is searching among bright gold threads
for a black pattern in the weave.

3

Set a string loop into a figure of two diamonds,
four diamonds, one diamond:
as a woman tightens her hand into a fist
and rubs it in a circular motion over her heart,
a bewildered man considering the semantics of *set*
decides no through-line exists:

to sink the head of a nail below the surface,
to fix as a distinguishing imprint, sign, or appearance,
to incite, put on a fine edge by grinding,
to adjust, adorn, put in motion, make unyielding,
to bend slightly the tooth points of a saw
alternately in opposite directions.

As the woman using her index finger makes
spiral after spiral from her aorta up over her head,
see the possibilities for transcendence:
you have to die and die in your mind
before you can begin to see the empty spaces
the configuration of string defines.

4

A restorer examines the pieces of a tin chandelier,
and notices the breaks in the arms are along
old solder lines, and that cheap epoxy was used.

He will have to scrape off the epoxy, scrub some flux,
heat up the chandelier and use a proper solder.
A pair of rough-legged hawks are circling over a pasture;

one hawk cuts off the rabbit's path of retreat
while the other swoops with sharp angle and curve of wings.
Cirrus, cirrostratus, cirrocumulus, altostratus,

altocumulus, stratocumulus, nimbostratus,
cumulus, cumulonimbus, stratus: is there no end?
Memories stored in the body begin to glow.

A woman seals basil in brown bags and hangs them
from the ceiling. A dead sturgeon washes to shore.
The sun is at the horizon, but another sun

is rippling in water. It's not that the angle
of reflection equals the angle of incidence,
but there's exultation, pleasure, distress, death, love.

5

The world resembles a cuttlefish changing colors
and shimmering. An apprentice archer has

stretched the bowstring properly, but does not know
he will miss the target because he is not aiming in the hips.

He will learn to hit the target without aiming
when he has died in his mind. I am not scared of death,

though I am appalled at how obsession with security
yields a pin-pushing, pencil-shaving existence.

You can descend to the swimming level of sharks,
be a giant kelp growing from the ocean bottom up

to the surface light, but the critical moment
is to die feeling the infinite stillness of the passions,

to revel in the touch of hips, hair, lips, hands,
feel the collapse of space in December light.

When I know I am no longer trying to know the spectral lines
of the earth, I can point to a cuttlefish and say,

"Here it is sepia," already it is deep-brown,
and exult, "Here it is deep-brown," already it is white.

6

Red koi swim toward us, and black
carp are rising out of the depths of the pond,
but our sustenance is a laugh, a grief,

a walk at night in the snow,
seeing the pure gold of a flickering candle—
a moment at dusk when we see

that deer have been staring at us,
we did not see them edge out of the brush,
a moment when someone turns on a light

and turns a window into a mirror,
a moment when a child asks,
"When will it be tomorrow?"

To say "A bell cannot be red and violet
at the same place and time because
of the logical structure of color" is true

but is a dot that must enlarge into
a zero: a void, *enso,* red shimmer,
breath, endless beginning, pure body, pure mind.

O

The Silk Road

1

The blood in your arteries is contaminated with sugar.
You may hate the adrenal reduction of the mind to

the mind of a dog, but *sic, run* may be forms of sugar.
You may whet for the smell of rain on a clear summer night.

You may whet for the sugar in red maple leaves.
You may whet for the blue needle of a compass to point

north, and when it points north insist you wanted it
to point north-northwest. No, yes. In a dream

you catch a white turtle in a net and a voice says,
"Kill it, divine with it, and you shall have good luck,"

but discard dream structure for a deeper asymmetry.
You thirst in your mind for an insulin, death:

death in the yellow saguaro flower opening at midnight,
death in a canyon wren's song at sunrise,

death in red carp swimming in a clear pool of water,
death in an April moonrise. Now the figure-of-eight knot,

overhand knot, thief knot, loop knot, bowline knot,
slide knot, slipknot, sheepshank is pulled tighter and tighter.

2

You may stare out of a south window for hours
and feel the April sunlight dissolve the shifting leaves,

and you may dream sunlight opening a red camellia.
You may eat monkey brains and bear paws,

but, out of disordered passions and a disordered mind,
can you construct yellow doors that open in silence into summer?

You may repeat mistake after mistake so that you
will the mistakes into an accelerating spiral of despair.

A turtle pushes onto the sand of Bikini Island,
and, disoriented by radiation, pushes farther and farther

inland to die; but do not confuse the bones
of a cow bleached in the sun with disordered desire.

You may dream sunlight shining into a cool mountain forest
and wake up inhaling the smell of Douglas fir.

You may dream sea turtles swimming in black water
but wake sunstruck walking in shifting dunes of white sand.

Who can say *here, now* is metempsychosic delusion?
Can you set out for Turfan today and arrive yesterday at dusk?

3

A man in a hospital is waiting for a heart transplant.
He may fish at night under the stars with a cool salt wind;

he may soar out over the black shining waters of a bay.
He may want to die with sunlight shining on his face;

he may want to die in a tsunami, but his yes and his no
are a void. He may die as a gray squirrel cracks open an acorn;

he may die as a green terrapin slips into a stream.
As a diabetic shivers and sweats, shivers and sweats,

he feels the moonlight shining on the high tide waters of the bay.
He feels the drone of traffic slip into silence, and then

the trivial, the inconsequential stings him, stings him.
As a child, he said to his father, "That man is weird;

why does he wear a pillow under his pants?" And his father laughed,
"He's fat, so fat." Then, "The Chinese word for onion

is *cong,* so a green onion is *xiao cong,* small onion, yes?"
"Yes." "Then a large white onion must be *da cong,* large

onion, yes?" "No, a large white onion is called *yang cong.*"
"*Yang cong*?" "Yes." "Which *yang*?" "The *yang* that means *ocean.*" "Shit."

4

The, a, this, the, tangerine, splash, hardly:
these threads of sound may be spun in s-spin into fiber:

lighted buoy, whistling buoy, spar buoy, bell buoy, buoy.
Hear the sounds of apricots dropping from branches to the earth;

feel the red vibration of wings before you see a hummingbird.
A man may travel from Mindanao to Macao to avoid

staring into himself; he may search at night in a helicopter
for the shimmer of a fire opal dropped into water;

he may inhale starlight as if it were a pungent yellow
flower opening slowly in the still August night.

To be still: watch a dog listen to sounds you cannot hear,
feel the pull of moonrise on the feathers of an owl.

There are apricots beginning to drop from branches to the earth;
there are apricots not yet beginning to drop from branches;

there are apricots not yet not yet beginning to drop.

5

This sand was black and silver shining in the megalight.
Now the radiation is in my hands and in your face.

You may dream red petals on a mountain path in rain;
I may watch the shimmer of light in the yellowing leaves.

Yes and no, spring and autumn have no power without the mind
that wills them into magnetic north, magnetic south.

A merchant from Xi'an brought ceremonial caps to Kuqa,
but the Kuqa people shaved their heads and tattooed their bodies.

To seal a dime in a red envelope and send it to
an insurance salesman is to send anthurium to a cannibal.

The taste of unripe persimmons, and pale moonlight shining
on the black hills appear to have no use: who

would have dreamed they would become, *shibui,* an aesthetic?
To argue that you must know the characteristic

that makes all birds birds before you can identify
a bird—and here you must discard antinomies—

postpones *auk* to that indeterminate time in the fallout
of the future when you shall have knowledge of the form *Death.*

6

Various proofs for the existence of God
try to predicate existence, but being

is unlike *yellow, sour, pungent.* That a branch
of the linden has yellow and dropping

leaves hardly enables us to infer that
water flowing through the underground *karez*

into Turfan is about to stop. If
the passions are the music of empty holes,

hear the blue and gold sounds of angst.
As I stared out the south window, I

saw the leaves of the linden green with no hint
of yellow. No, as I stared out the south

window, I wanted to see the yellowing leaves,
but instead saw, reflected in the glass

back through the space of the room
and out another window, salted skates

hanging on a wire to dry. So what I saw
reflected deflected my intention as now I say *now.*

O

Oolong

1

Tea leaves wilted in sunlight are shaken
and bruised so that the edges redden
and veins turn transparent. A man at a counter
eats boiled silk worms and coughs;
a woman stops speaking and stares
at the constellation Perseus. Once,
a merchant smashed a black raku bowl
when it failed to please a tea master,
but, glued back together, the black shards
had the texture of mulberry leaves.
You pass someone bowing talking on the telephone,
and the shock is an incandescent quark
leaving a spiraling track in the mind:
you sense how, in a field guide, it is impossible
to know the growth arc of a mushroom,
but stumble upon shelves of oysters
growing out of dead aspens and
see how nothing in this world is yet yours.

2

True or false:

termites release methane and add to the greenhouse effect;

the skin of a blowfish is lethal;

crosses along roads in Mexico mark vehicular deaths;

the earth is flat;

oysters at full moon contain hepatitis;

no one has ever seen a neutrino;

butterflies dream;

the fins of a blowfish are always edible;

oolong means *black dragon,* but *oo* means *crow* and *long* means *dragon;*

he loved the curves of her body;

the sun revolves around the earth;

caffeine stimulates the central nervous system;

light is a wave;

the mind is composed of brightest bright and darkest dark;

context is crucial;

pfennigs, xu, qindarka, centimes, stotinki, qursh are coins;

the raw liver of a tiger blowfish
caught at winter solstice is a delicacy;

I have a knife inscribed with the names of forty-eight fish.

3

You sift curtains of red light
shimmering in the November sky,
sift the mind of a roofer mopping hot tar.
Walking down a hallway, you stop

and sift the brains in a glass bowl,
sift the tag dangling from the wrist of a corpse,
sift the folded wings of a sparrow.
The prevailing notions of the season

are green-stained lactarius prevailing
in the mountains for three days and an hour.
You have to reject ideas of disjunction
and collage, reject advice, praise.

Then you might look at a Song dynasty map
of Hangzhou and see the configuration
of ion channels in the brain. You might look
at an aboriginal sand painting and see

a cosmology of grief. You might look
at the swaying motion of a branch
and feel what it is to be a
burned and shriveled leaf clinging to death.

4

I stare into a black bowl and smell
whisked green tea, see a flap of tails
and orange koi surging in a stream.
Sunlight is dropping down through tallest pines;
I stop on a bridge, and water
passes underneath and through me.
As a potter has a premonition of death
when he avoids using a red glaze on a square dish,
we come to know the form and pressure of an emotion
when it's gone: a soliloquy of despair
ends as a rope burn in the hands,
and pleasure flares into a gold chrysanthemum.
Is the spinning spinless when nothing is yours?
The mind slows to a green-flecked swirl;
I touch contours of the black shards.
Before sunrise, a man is cutting all
the morning glories blooming in the garden
and places one in a jar in a tearoom.

5

They smuggled his corpse into the city in a pile of rotting abalone;

"Very famous": they all nodded;

he knew the daphne was a forbidden flower;

"Twerp," a restaurant inspector muttered
and placed a C in the window;

they slurped noodles and read comic books;

he spits off the subway platform;

the slightest noise so disturbed him he had a soundproof room built:
white walls, white floor;

she kept feeling a snail on her neck;

for tea ceremony,
he cut three gentians and threw them into an Acoma pot;

she buried the placenta in the cornfield;

a hunter discovers a honey mushroom larger than a blue whale;

what opens and closes, closes and opens?

she took his breath away;

he dips his brush
and writes the character *flower* incorporating the character *mind;*

a flayed elephant skin;

she stir-fries tea leaves in a wok.

6

Red poppies are blooming along a wall;
I look at green and underlying blue paint
peeling off a bench: you rummage in a shed
and find a spindle, notice the oil of
hands has accumulated on the shaft.
In the rippling shadows, the shimmer of water.
I see yellow irises in a vase on the kitchen table
and smell lightning; commuters at the World
Trade Center may descend escalators to subways:
it is always 5:05; Su-wei brought him
five thousand yellow pills and said if
he swallowed twelve each day it would
restore his hair, but is this a form of
sipping sake steeped in a jar full of vipers?
Footprints underwater in a rice paddy
and on the water's surface, clouds;
Altair and Vega spin in longing:
the sun dips below the horizon in a watery gold.

7

The mycelium of a honey mushroom
glows in the dark. What does a yellow
Man On Horseback know of winter and spring?
A farmer pushes his fist into clay

and forms a bowl. The world will continue
as long as two aborigines
clack boomerangs and chant?
A woman has the watery shine

of a sapphire and becomes yellow lightning.
She has a dream that resembles a geode:
if we could open it we might
recover the hue of the first world.

The light through a pressed octopus cup
has a rippling texture resembling
a cool undulating shadow over skin.
In the dark, the precession

and nutation of an emotion is a star:
Sirius, Arcturus, Capella, Procyon, Aldebaran:
shadows of mosquitoes are moving
along a rice-paper screen.

O

In Your Honor

In your honor, a man presents a sea bass
tied to a black-lacquered dish by green-spun seaweed.

"Ah" is heard throughout the room:
you are unsure what is about to happen.

You might look through a telescope at the full
bright moon against deep black space,

see from the Bay of Dew to the Sea of Nectar,
but this beauty of naming is a subterfuge.

What are the thoughts of hunters driving
home on a Sunday afternoon empty-handed?

Their conception of honor may coincide
with your conception of cruelty? The slant

of light as sun declines is a knife
separating will and act into infinitely thin

and lucid slices. You look at the sea bass's eye,
clear and luminous. The gills appear to move

ever so slightly. The sea bass smells
of dream, but this is no dream. "Ah,

such delicacy" is heard throughout the room,
and the sea bass suddenly flaps. It

bleeds and flaps, bleeds and flaps as
the host slices slice after slice of glistening sashimi.

The Flower Path

Down to the north end of this veranda, behind the view
of 1,001 gold-leafed statues of Kuan-yin looking east,
Wasa Daihachiro, in twenty-four hours in 1686, shot
13,054 arrows of which 8,133 were bull's-eyes. Today
no one can pull the two-hundred-pound laminated bamboo bow
to send a single arrow with a low trajectory the length
of the thirty-three bays. As you walk on the veranda,
you see a tree full of white bags tied over peaches,
hear the sound of bells at a fish auction,
note the stares of men sitting on tiers under lights;
you are careful not to raise your hand as you examine
a two-hundred-pound tuna smoking just unpacked from dry ice;
at lunch you put a shrimp in your mouth and feel it twitch;
you enter a house and are dazed as your eyes adjust to
a hundred blind Darumas in the room;
you must learn to see a pond in the shape of the character *mind,*
walk through a garden and see it from your ankles;
a family living behind a flower-arrangement shop
presents the store as a face to the street;
the eldest daughter winces when the eighty-year-old parents
get out wedding pictures of the second daughter;
at night the belching sounds of frogs;
in the morning you look in rice paddies and find only tadpoles;
you are walking down into a gorge along the river,
turn to find stone-piled-on-stone offerings along the path
and on rocks in midstream; in the depths of the cave,
a gold mirror with candles burning;
deer running at dusk in a dry moat;
irises blooming and about to bloom;
you are walking across Moon-Crossing Bridge in slashing rain,
meet a Rinzai monk with a fax machine
who likes to crank up a Victrola with a gold horn;
you see the red-ochre upper walls of a teahouse,
and below the slatted bamboo fences called "dog repellers";
you stop at the south end of the veranda and look north;
an actor walks off the flower-path ramp cross-eyed amid shouts.

The Great White Shark

For days he has dumped a trail of tuna blood
into the ocean so that a great white shark

might be lured, so that we might touch its fin.
The power of the primitive is parallactic:

in a museum exhibit, a *chacmool* appears as elegant
and sophisticated sculpture, as art, but

witness the priest rip the still-beating heart
out of the blue victim's body and place it

pulsing on a *chacmool* and we are ready to vomit.
We think the use of a beryllium gyroscope

marks technological superiority, but the urge
of ideologies then and now makes revenge inexorable.

The urge to skydive, rappel, white-water kayak
is the urge to release, the urge to die.

Diamond and graphite may be allotropic forms
of carbon, but what are the allotropic forms

of ritual and desire? The moon shining on black water,
yellow forsythia blossoming in the April night,

red maple leaves dropping in silence in October:
the seasons are not yet human forms of desire.

Slanting Light

Slanting light casts onto a stucco wall
the shadows of upwardly zigzagging plum branches.

I can see the thinning of branches to the very twig.
I have to sift what you say, what she thinks,

what he believes is genetic strength, what
they agree is inevitable. I have to sift this

quirky and lashing stillness of form to see myself,
even as I see laid out on a table for Death

an assortment of pomegranates and gourds.
And what if Death eats a few pomegranate seeds?

Does it ensure a few years of pungent spring?
I see one gourd, yellow from midsection to top

and zucchini-green lower down, but
already the big orange gourd is gnawed black.

I have no idea why the one survives the killing nights.
I have to sift what you said, what I felt,

what you hoped, what I knew. I have to sift
death as the stark light sifts the branches of the plum.

Red Octopus

She folds the four corners into the center,
hears the sound of a porcupine in a cornfield,
smells heart-shaped leaves in the dark.
She stops, noticing she has folded the red side out.
She is supposed to fold so that the red is seen
through white as what lies below surface.

So she restarts and folds the creases in air.
She recalls her mother arguing and flashing her party card;
she recalls soldiers at the Great Hall of the People
receiving medals; she recalls her father filming
a chimpanzee smoking a cigarette at the Beijing zoo;
she senses how the soldiers were betrayed.

She makes a petal fold, a valley fold,
an open-sink fold, a series of mountain folds,
pondering how truths were snared by malice.
She makes an inside-reverse fold, crimps the legs,
and, with a quick spurt of air,
inflates the body of the octopus.

Whiteout

You expect to see swirling chunks of ice
flowing south toward open water of the ocean,
but, no, a moment of whiteout as
the swirling ice flows north at sunset.
In a restaurant with an empty screen,
a woman gets up and sings a Chinese song
with "empty orchestra" accompaniment.
Prerecorded music fills the room,
and projection from a laser disc throws
a waterfall and red hibiscus onto the screen.
You are not interested in singing and
following the words as they change color
from yellow to purple across the cueing machine.
Instead, you walk out on blue-green glacier
ice and feel it thin to water in spring.
You notice two moose along the thawing shoreline
browsing for buds, and see the posted sign
No Shooting From Here. But "here" is "there."

Ice Floe

Nails dropped off a roof onto flagstone;
slow-motion shatter of a windowpane;
the hushed sound when a circular saw cutting through plywood
stops, and splinters of wood are drifting in air;
lipstick graffiti on a living-room wall;
cold stinging your eardrums;
braking suddenly along a curve, and the car spinning,
holding your breath as the side-view mirror is snapped by a sign pole;
the snap as a purple chalk line marks an angular cut on black Cellutex;
dirt under your nails,
as you dig up green onions with your bare hands;
fiber plaster setting on a wall;
plugging in an iron and noticing the lights dim in the other room;
sound of a pencil drawn along the edge of a trisquare;
discovering your blurred vision is caused by having two contacts in each eye;
thud as the car slams into a snowbank and hits a fence;
smell of a burnt yam;
the bones of your wrist being crushed;
under a geranium leaf, a mass of spiders
moving slowly on tiny threads up and down and across to different stems.

The Los Alamos Museum

In this museum are replicas of Little Boy and Fat Man. In Little Boy, a radar echo set off an explosive which drove a uranium-235 wedge into a larger uranium target, while in Fat Man the ordinary explosive crushed a hollow sphere of plutonium into a beryllium core. To the right of these replicas, a computer gives you the opportunity to design a reentry missile out of aluminum or steel. The reentry point of the aluminum missile needs to be thicker than the steel one, but, because it has a lighter atomic weight, when you push the button choosing the aluminum design, the computer rewards you with blinking lights and sounds. Farther on in the main room, a model with lights shows the almost instantaneous release of neutrons and gamma rays from point zero. At point zero, radiant energy is released at the speed of light, but you can see it here in slow motion.

Spring Snow

A spring snow coincides with plum blossoms.
In a month, you will forget, then remember
when nine ravens perched in the elm sway in wind.

I will remember when I brake to a stop,
and a hubcap rolls through the intersection.
An angry man grinds pepper onto his salad;

it is how you nail a tin amulet ear
into the lintel. If, in deep emotion, we are
possessed by the idea of possession,

we can never lose to recover what is ours.
Sounds of an abacus are amplified and condensed
to resemble sounds of hail on a tin roof,

but mind opens to the smell of lightning.
Bodies were vaporized to shadows by intense heat;
in memory people outline bodies on walls.

O

The Redshifting Web

1

The dragons on the back of a circular bronze mirror
swirl without end. I sit and am an absorbing form:
I absorb the outline of a snowy owl on a branch,
the rigor mortis in a hand. I absorb the crunching sounds
when you walk across a glacial lake with aquamarine
ice heaved up here and there twenty feet high.
I absorb the moment a jeweler pours molten gold
into a cuttlefish mold and it begins to smoke.
I absorb the weight of a pause when it tilts
the conversation in a room. I absorb the moments
he sleeps holding her right breast in his left hand
and know it resembles glassy waves in a harbor
in descending spring light. Is the mind a mirror?
I see pig carcasses piled up from the floor
on a boat docked at Wanxian and the cook
who smokes inadvertently drops ashes into soup.
I absorb the stench of burning cuttlefish bone,
and as moments coalesce see to travel far is to return.

2

A cochineal picker goes blind;

Mao, swimming across the Yangtze River,
was buoyed by underwater frogmen;

in the nursing home,
she yelled, "Everyone here has Alzheimer's!"

it blistered his mouth;

they thought the tape of erhu solos was a series of spy messages;

finding a bag of piki pushpinned to the door;

shapes of saguaros by starlight;

a yogi tries on cowboy boots at a flea market;

a peregrine falcon
shears off a wing;

her niece went through the house and took what she wanted;

"the sooner the better";

like a blindman grinding the bones of a snow leopard;

she knew you had come to cut her hair;

suffering: this and that:
iron 26, gold 79;

they dared him to stare at the annular eclipse;

the yellow pupils of a saw-whet owl.

3

The gold shimmer at the beginning of summer
dissolves in a day. A fly mistakes a
gold spider, the size of a pinhead, at the center
of a glistening web. A morning mushroom
knows nothing of twilight and dawn?
Instead of developing a navy, Ci Xi
ordered architects to construct a two-story
marble boat that floats on a lotus-covered lake.
Mistake a death cap for Caesar's amanita
and in hours a hepatic hole opens into the sky.
To avoid yelling at his pregnant wife,
a neighbor installs a boxing bag in a storeroom;
he periodically goes in, punches, punches,
reappears and smiles. A hummingbird moth
hovers and hovers at a woman wearing a
cochineal-dyed flowery dress. Liu Hansheng
collects hypodermic needles, washes them
under a hand pump, dries them in sunlight,
seals them in Red Cross plastic bags,
resells them as sterilized new ones to hospitals.

4

Absorb a corpse-like silence and be a brass
cone at the end of a string beginning
to mark the x of stillness. You may puzzle
as to why a meson beam oscillates, or why
galaxies appear to be simultaneously redshifting
in all directions, but do you stop to sense
death pulling and pulling from the center
of the earth to the end of the string?
A mother screams at her son, "You're so stupid,"
but the motion of this anger is a circle.
A teen was going to attend a demonstration,
but his parents, worried about tear gas,
persuaded him to stay home: he was bludgeoned
to death that afternoon by a burglar.
I awake dizzy with a searing headache
thinking what nightmare did I have
that I cannot remember only to discover
the slumlord dusted the floor with roach powder.

5

On a tanker moored off Qingdao, the pilot
sells dismantled bicycles before sunrise.
Once, a watchmaker coated numbers on the dial

with radioactive paint and periodically
straightened the tip of the brush in his mouth.
Our son sights the North Star through a straw

taped to a protractor so that a bolt
dangling from a string marks the latitude.
I remember when he said his first word, "Clock";

his 6:02 is not mine, nor is your 7:03 his.
We visit Aurelia in the nursing home and find
she is sleeping curled in a fetal position.

A chain-smoking acupuncturist burps, curses;
a teen dips his head in paint thinner.
We think, had I *this* then that would,

but subjunctive form is surge and ache.
Yellow tips of chamisa are flaring open.
I drop a jar of mustard, and it shatters in a wave.

6

The smell of roasted chile;

descending into the epilimnion;

the shape of a datura leaf;

a bank robber superglued his fingertips;

in the lake,
ocean-seal absorption;

a moray snaps up a scorpion fish;

he had to mistake and mistake;

burned popcorn;

he lifted the fly agaric off of blue paper
and saw a white galaxy;

sitting in a cold sweat;

a child drinking Coke out of a formula bottle
has all her teeth capped in gold;

chrysanthemum-shaped fireworks exploding over the water;

red piki passed down a ladder;

laughter;

as a lobster mold transforms a russula into a delicacy;

replicating an Anasazi
yucca fiber and turkey-feather blanket.

7

He looks at a series of mirrors: Warring States,
Western Han, Eastern Han, Tang, Song,
and notices bits of irregular red corrosion

on the Warring States mirror. On the back,
three dragons swirl in mist and April air.
After sixteen years that first kiss

still has a flaring tail. He looks at the TLV
pattern on the back of the Han mirror:
the mind has diamond points east, south, west, north.

He grimaces and pulls up a pile of potatoes,
notices snow clouds coming in from the west.
She places a sunflower head on the northwest

corner of the fence. He looks at the back
of the Tang mirror: the lion and grape
pattern is so wrought he turns, watches her

pick eggplant, senses the underlying
twist of pleasure and surprise that
in mind they flow and respond endlessly.

8

I find a rufous hummingbird on the floor
of a greenhouse, sense a redshifting
along the radial string of a web.
You may draw a cloud pattern in cement
setting in a patio, or wake to
sparkling ferns melting on a windowpane.
The struck, plucked, bowed, blown
sounds of the world come and go.
As first light enters a telescope
and one sees light of a star when the star
has vanished, I see a finch at a feeder,
beans germinating in darkness;
a man with a pole pulls yarn out
of an indigo vat, twists and untwists it;
I hear a shout as a child finds *Boletus*
barrowsii under ponderosa pine;
I see you wearing an onyx-and-gold pin.
In curved space, is a line a circle?

9

Pausing in the motion of a stroke,
two right hands
grasping a brush;

    staring through a skylight
    at a lunar eclipse;

a great blue heron,
wings flapping,
landing on the rail of a float house;

    near and far:
    a continuous warp;

a neighbor wants to tear down this fence;
a workman covets it
for a *trastero;*

    raccoons on the rooftop
    eating apricots;

the character *xuan*—
dark, dyed—
pinned to a wall above a computer;

    lovers making
    a room glow;

weaving on a vertical loom:
sound of a comb,
baleen;

    hiding a world in a world:
    1054, a supernova.

O

X-Ray

In my mind a lilac begins to leaf

before it begins to leaf.
A new leaf

is a new moon.
As the skin of a chameleon

reflects temperature, light, emotion,
an X-ray of my hands

reflects chance, intention, hunger?
You can, in X-ray
diffraction,
study the symmetry of crystals,

but here, now,
the caesura marks a shift in the mind,

the vicissitudes
of starlight,

a luna moth opening its wings.

Rattlesnake Glyph

Curve of the earth in emerald water
deepening into blue where water breaks along

the outer edge of a reef. A snake of equinoctial
light is beginning to descend the nine tiers

of a pyramid. You hear a shout reverberate
down the walls of a ball court, find blood

snakes spurting out of the neck of a decapitated man,
the carved stone ring through which a human head

used as a ball must pass. Here is a wall of
a thousand white sculptured-stone skulls

and row after row of heads mounted on spikes.
The darkness drops a mosquito net over a bed:

in blood-scroll skull light, I taste the salt
on your skin and in your hair. We are

a rattlesnake glyph aligning memory, dream, desire.
At dawn the slashing sounds of rain turn out

to be wind in the palms. Waves are breaking white
on the reef. Soon turtles will arrive and lay

eggs in the sand. Leaf-cutting ants in a line
are passing bits of shiny green leaves across a trail.

A Great Square Has No Corners

"Cut."
An actress feigning death for one hundred seconds gasps.
A man revs
and races a red Mustang up and down the street.
"Cut."

A potter opens a hillside kiln;
he removes a molten bowl,
and, dipping it
in cold water,
it hisses, turns black, cracks.

In despair, a pearl is a sphere.
"Cut."
In Bombay, a line of ear cleaners are standing in a street.
On a mesa top,
the south windows of a house shatter;

underground uranium miners
are releasing explosives.
"Cut."
A rope beginning to unravel in the mind
is, like red antlers,

the axis of a dream.
"Cut."
What is the secret to stopping time?
A one-eyed calligrapher
writes with a mop, "A great square has no corners."

Axolotl

I may practice divination with the bones
of an eel, but the world would be
just as cruel were it within my will.

The yellowing leaves of the honey locust
would still be yellowing, and a woman
riding in a hearse would still grieve and grieve.

We don't live in a hypothetical world,
and yet the world would be nothing
without hypothetical dreaming. I hope no

ultimate set of laws to nature exists;
maybe, instead, there's only layering.
Maybe you look in a store window and see

twenty-four televisions with twenty-four images:
now the explosion of a napalm bomb,
now the face of an axolotl.

Mushroom Hunting in the Jemez Mountains

Walking in a mountain meadow toward the north slope,
I see redcap amanitas with white warts and know
they signal cèpes. I see a few colonies of puffballs,
red russulas with chalk-white stipes, brown-gilled
Poison Pie. In the shade under spruce are two
red-pored boletes: slice them in half and the flesh
turns blue in seconds. Under fir is a single amanita
with basal cup, flaring annulus, white cap: is it
the Rocky Mountain form of *Amanita pantherina*?
I am aware of danger in naming, in misidentification,
in imposing the distinctions of a taxonomic language
onto the things themselves. I know I have only
a few hours to hunt mushrooms before early afternoon rain.
I know it is a mistake to think I am moving and
that agarics are still: they are more transient
than we acknowledge, more susceptible to full moon,
to a single rain, to night air, to a moment of sunshine.
I know in this meadow my passions are mycorrhizal
with nature. I may shout out ecstasies, aches, griefs,
and hear them vanish in the white-pored silence.

From the Rooftop

He wakes up to the noise of ravens in the spruce trees.
For a second, in the mind, the parsley is already
bolting in the heat, but then he realizes
the mind focusing rays into a burning point of light
can also relax its intensity, and then
he feels the slow wave of the day.
Mullein growing by the gas meter
is as significant as the portulaca blooming in pots.
Ants are marching up the vine onto the stucco wall
and into the roof. From the rooftop,
he contemplates the pattern of lightning to the west,
feels a nine-pointed buck edge closer to the road at dusk,
weighs a leaf and wonders what is significant,
maybe the neighbor who plays the saxophone
at odd hours, loudly and badly, but with such expanse.

The Shapes of Leaves

Ginkgo, cottonwood, pin oak, sweet gum, tulip tree:
our emotions resemble leaves and alive
to their shapes we are nourished.

Have you felt the expanse and contours of grief
along the edges of a big Norway maple?
Have you winced at the orange flare

searing the curves of a curling dogwood?
I have seen from the air logged islands,
each with a network of branching gravel roads,

and felt a moment of pure anger, aspen gold.
I have seen sandhill cranes moving in an open field,
a single white whooping crane in the flock.

And I have traveled along the contours
of leaves that have no name. Here
where the air is wet and the light is cool,

I feel what others are thinking and do not speak,
I know pleasure in the veins of a sugar maple,
I am living at the edge of a new leaf.

O

Original Memory

1

White orchids along the window—
she notices something has nibbled the eggplant leaves,

mantises have not yet hatched from the egg.
"*Traduttori, traditori,*" said a multilinguist

discussing the intricacies of Hopi time and space,
but the inadvertent resonance in the mind

is that passion is original memory:
she is at the window pointing to Sagittarius,

she is slicing porcini and laying them in a pan,
she is repotting a cereus wearing chalcedony and gold earrings,

she is judging kachinas and selecting the simplest
to the consternation of museum employees.

Grilled shrimp in olive oil—
a red sensation pours into his thought and touch:

the sfumato of her face,
shining black hair reaching down to her waist,

he knows without looking the plum
bruises on her thigh from the spikes of a sectional warp.

2

The multilinguist wants to reveal the locations
of shrines on the salt trail in the Grand Canyon

but has been declared persona non grata by the tribe.
He may have disproved the thesis that the Hopi language

has no referents to time, but his obsession led
to angers and accusations, betrayals and pentimenti:

a cry of a nuthatch vanishes into aquamarine air.
Some things you have to see by making a pinhole,

holding a white sheet of paper at the proper focal length?
To try to retrace the arc of a passion is to

try to dream in slow motion a bursting into flame?
You are collecting budding yellow tea plants;

I am feeling a sexual splendor in a new orchid leaf.
What is the skin of the mind?

How do you distinguish "truth" from "true perception"?
When is an apex a nadir and a nadir an opening into a first world?

Italians slice porcini, lay them on screens in the sun,
let the maggots wriggle out and drop to the ground.

3

She is tipping water out of a cloud.
By candlelight, face to face;

the pleasures of existence are caught in a string of pearls.
He remembers her rhythm in a corn dance,

notices the swelling of her left ear from a new earring.
He does not want any distortion—

red leaves falling or beginning to fall,
bright yellow chamisa budding along a dirt road,

snow accumulating on black branches—
to this moment of chiaroscuro in which their lives are a sphere.

Face to face, by candlelight;
the rockwork and doorways form a series of triptychs.

She remembers hiking the trail up to Peñasco Blanco,
sees the Chuska Mountains violet in the west,

and, below, the swerve of Chaco Wash,
the canyon opening up: ruins of rock walls

calcined in the heat, and, in red light,
swallows gathering and daubing mud along the cliff face.

o

Archipelago

1

I walk along the length of a stone-and-gravel garden
and feel without looking how the fifteen stones
appear and disappear. I had not expected the space
to be defined by a wall made of clay boiled in oil
nor to see above a series of green cryptomeria
pungent in spring. I stop and feel an April snow
begin to fall on the stones and raked gravel and see
how distance turns into abstraction desire and ordinary
things: from the air, corn and soybean fields are
a series of horizontal and vertical stripes of pure color:
viridian, yellow ochre, raw sienna, sap green. I
remember in Istanbul at the entrance to the Blue Mosque
two parallel, extended lines of shoes humming at
the threshold of paradise. Up close, it's hard to know
if the rattle of milk bottles will become a topaz,
or a moment of throttled anger tripe that is
chewed and chewed. In the distance, I feel drumming
and chanting and see a line of Pueblo women dancing
with black-on-black jars on their heads; they lift
the jars high then start to throw them to the ground.

2

Rope at ankle level,
a walkway sprinkled with water
under red and orange maples along a white-plastered wall;

moss covering the irregular ground
under propped-up weeping cherry trees;

in a corral
a woman is about to whisper and pat the roan's neck;

an amber chasm inside a cello;

in a business conversation,
the silences are eel farms passed on a bullet train;

a silence in the shape of a rake;

a sheet of ice floating along a dock;
the texture of icy-black basil leaves at sunrise;

a shaggymane pushing up through asphalt;

a woman wearing a multicolored dress of silk-screened naked women
about to peel an egg;

three stones leading into a pond.

3

Desire is to memory as an azalea is to a stone?
During the Cultural Revolution, the youngest brother
of the Peng family was executed against a wall
in Chengdu for being a suspected Guomindang agent.
Years earlier, the eldest brother was executed
at that wall for being a suspected communist.
This Chengdu effect has no end, but if you interiorize,
a series of psychological tragedies
has the resonance of stone-and-gravel waterfalls.
A first frost sweetens the apples; I want them sweeter
but discover a second frost makes the cores mush;
so essential shapes are destroyed starting at the center.
A woman and man must ache from a series of betrayals
before they can begin to bicker at the dinner table.
I water hyacinth bulbs planted in shallow pots
in the cool, dark bathroom, and, though it feels
odd to do so when walnuts are rotting on the ground,
a thought of spring is inadvertent pleasure:
a policeman pushed a dancer against a car, said, "Sure,"
when he insisted he had marigolds, not marijuana.

4

She puts jars in a pit, covers them with sawdust,
adds a layer of shards and covers them,
builds a fire, and, when the burn is intense,
smothers it with sheep dung. She will not know
for a few hours if the jars have turned completely
black and did not break cooling. For now,
no one sees or knows; I inhale smoke, see
vendors along the docks selling grilled
corn smelling of charcoal, the air at dusk
plangent with cries from minarets up on the hill—
the cries resembling the waves of starlings
that always precede the pulsing wing-beat Vs
of sandhill cranes. Oh, you can glow with anger,
but it leaves the soot of an oil burner
on the windows and walls. If anguish is an end
in itself, you walk into a landscape of
burned salt cedar along a river. I remember
seeing hungry passengers disembark at the docks.

5

Men dressed in cottonwood leaves dance
in the curving motion of a green rattlesnake.
I am walking along a sandstone trail
and stop in a field of shards: here is a teal zigzag
and there is a bloodred deer's breath-arrow.
Women dancers offer melons to the six directions
then throw them to the ground. A wave
rocks through the crowd as the melons are smashed open.
I know I have walked along a path lit
by candles inside open-mesh cast-iron carp.
I stop at a water basin, and as I bend to
ladle water, see reflected a sweet-gum leaf.
As a cornmeal path becomes a path to the gods
then a cornmeal path again, I see the line
of women dancing with black-on-black jars on their heads.
They raise the jars with macaw and lightning patterns
to the six directions then form a circle
and throw them down on the center-marking stones.

6

"Go kiss a horse's ass."

"He hanged himself from the flagpole."

"I just do what I'm told."

She wanted him to hold her and say nothing.

"Depression is due to loss or guilt."

Who heard shrieks?
In the morning,
a mutilated body was found behind the adobe church.

He saw that "A or B" was not a choice since A and B had been predetermined.

"I hated that painting painting so I burned it."

Hair on the woodstove.

"I'm so glad."

After fallopian surgery, she touches her scar, combs her hair, puts on makeup.

The red phoenix tattoos on the arms of a locksmith.

"A man's character is his fate."

He had two cameras but was always pawning one to release the other.

They slept a Mediterranean sleep: sun, sand, water;
the bed had the soft motion of waves.

"No, no, no, no, no, no, no!"

"Water is the koan of water."

7

I look at fourteen stones submerged at varying depths
in a sea of gravel. I do not know under which stone
is a signature but guess that a pin-sized hourglass space,
separating intention and effect, is a blind point
where anger may coalesce into a pearl. I may sit here
until the stones have a riparian shine and are buoyant
in September starlight, yet never live to see
how grief turns into the effortless stretch of a fisherman
casting a fly onto a stream. When I slept on the float house
I became accustomed to the rise and fall of the tide,
so that when I walked on the rain forest island
I was queasy. I wanted a still pellucid point
but realize the necessary and sufficient condition
is to feel the pin-sized space as a point of resistance,
as a smash that is a beginning wave of light.
The dancers reappear and enter the plaza in two lines.
Shifting feet in rhythm to the shifting drumming,
they approach the crowd under the yellow cottonwood.

8

Mating above the cattails, red dragonflies—

sipping lychee tea, eating fried scallion pancakes—

bamboo slivers under the fingernails—

playing Ping-Pong by candlelight in a greenhouse—

digging up and rotating soil in the flower beds—

pulling and pulling at her throat until it bleeds—

scraping the skin of the earth—

finding shaggymanes have deliquesced into black ink—

releasing endorphins in the brain—

archipelago:
an expanse of water with many scattered islands—

a python coiling around sixteen white oblong eggs—

waking in the dark to pungent hyacinths—

blooming the pure white curve of blooming—

dancers are throwing
licorice, sunflower seeds, pot scrubbers, aprons, plastic bowls.

9

Plastic bowls, aprons, pot scrubbers, sunflower seeds, licorice—

the shadow of a hummingbird—

crab apple blossoms scattering in the street—

a silence in the shape of a chanterelle—

a turkey feather hanging from a branch of mountain ash—

the forms of lightning—

a yellow iris blooming near the house marker, 1932—

river stones marking the noon solstice—

black, *blak, blæc*—

following the thread
of recollection through a lifetime—

the passions becoming the chiming sounds of jade—

blue corn growing in a field of sand—

the *chug chug, ka ka* of a cactus wren—

a black-and-yellow butterfly closing then opening its wings—

egrets wading in shallow water at low tide.

Quipu

2005

quipu \'kē-(ˌ)pü\ *n* [Sp *quipo,* fr. Quechua *khipu*] (1704) : a device made of a main cord with smaller varicolored cords attached and knotted and used by the ancient Peruvians (as for calculating)

Merriam-Webster's Collegiate Dictionary

Before Sunrise

The myriad unfolds from a progression of strokes—
one, ice, corpse, hair, jade, tiger.

Unlocking a gate along a barbed-wire fence,
I notice beer cans and branches in the acequia.

There are no white pear blossoms by the gate,
no red poppies blooming in the yard,

no *Lepiota naucina* clustered by the walk,
but—bean, gold—there's the intricacy of a moment

when—wind, three-legged incense cauldron—
I begin to walk through a field with cow pies

toward the Pojoaque River, sense deer, *yellow,* rat.
I step through water, go up the arroyo, find

a dark green magpie feather. This is a time
when—blood in my piss, ache in nose and teeth—

I sense tortoise, flute where there is no sound,
wake to human bones carved and strung into a loose apron.

Earthshine

1

"Fuck you, *fuck you,*" he repeated as he drove down the dirt road
while tamarisk branches scraped the side of the pickup;

what scrapes in the mind as it dilates to darkness?

"*Jodido,*" he winced and turned up the whites of his eyes;

"What comes from darkness, I strike with darkness";

who hears a night-blooming cereus
unfold a white blossom by the windowsill?

crackle of flames in the fireplace;

lapping of waves against rocks
as a manta ray flips and feeds on plankton;

the gasp when he glanced down at the obituaries;

the gasp when she unwrapped flecked rice paper to find a letterpress broadside;

spurt of match into gold as he lights white beeswax candles;

she is running her hair between his toes;
he is rubbing her nipples with his palms;

"What comes from brightness, I strike with brightness";

his ankles creaked as he tiptoed to the bathroom;

waking to a cat chewing on a mouse in the dark.

2

Hiking up a trail in the Manoa Valley arboretum,
he motions with his hand to stop as he tries
to distinguish whether a red-whiskered or
red-vented bulbul has just landed on a branch.
I spot a macadamia nut on the ground, glance
up into an adjacent tree and am shocked by
two enormous jackfruit suspended from the trunk.
Revelation never comes as a fern uncoiling
a frond in mist; it comes when I trip on a root,
slap a mosquito on my arm. We go on, but stop
when gnats lift into a cloud as we stumble into
a bunch of rose apples rotting on the ground.
Although we continue to a dead end where water
runs down a sheer rock, the mind stops here:
here *Amanita muscaria*s release a cloud of spores
into cool August air; here lovers make
earthshine on a waxing crescent moon; here
the phone rings and I learn of a suicide,
a pinhole grows into an eclipse; here
water drips as I descend into a sloping black lava tube.

3

Say teeth;
say gnawed his teeth in his sleep;
say each spring he scraped peeling blue paint off the windowsill;
say the ocean flickers;
say a squiggly chalk line screeching down a blackboard opens a black rift;
say on a float house yellow cedar smoke rises in the woodstove;
say burn;
say crumpled white papers ripple then burst into yellow twists of flame;
say parallel lines touch in the infinite;
say peel;
say stoplight screech go green laugh;
say screech, rip, slam, thud, body scrapes, bleeds to bone;
say hyena;
say bobcat stripped of skin;
say a black cricket chirps in a corner of the room;
say hang;
say ox shoulder hangs off hook;
say trimming roses, she slashed her left wrist;
say shit-smear hair-sway leaf-gold ooze;
say crack;
say breaking a wineglass in a white napkin recovers a sliver of original light;
say egg-white eyeball splash;
say rinse;
say bend to earth, find a single stalk budding gold.

4

He hanged himself with his belt in the bosque
is no longer a whip that reddens and flays the skin.
"Donkey piss," he once cracked—but who
knows how the light sizzled and burned a hole
that gnawed and gnawed so that the more he
twisted the more he convulsed into a black pitch?
Orange daylilies are blooming along the driveway;
long-stalked delphinium are bending to earth.
A firework explodes in white-gold then bursts
into a green shimmer. He leaves teeth marks
on her neck; she groans and shows the whites
of her eyes. When a car rushes by on a wet road,
he hears a laborer throw sand against a tilted screen
and realizes twenty-three years ago he threw
sand against a tilted screen. Now, when he
strokes the tendons of her left wrist, she sighs.
They are nowhere everywhere nonesuch;
they are not *look back time* but full moon first light.

5

She said he said "moon" in his sleep;

when he looked through the potbellied telescope,
the light of the full moon made him wince;

he had to gaze into darkness
and then saw from Mare Cognitum to Mare Serenitatis;

the mind aches to see at such distance such definition;

when she heard the barking dog,
she shined a flashlight and spotted a porcupine on the roof;

as you would spotlight a deer;

a snake slides under the redwood boardwalk by the kitchen;

he kisses her shoulders,
rubs the soles of her feet;

the mind aligns such slivers;

say dragonfly, quartz, cattail, tuning fork, wave;
say earthstar bursting into alpine air;
say c^2;

say even the sacred barley drink separates if it is not stirred,
and see how, stirred, one can find repose.

6

Sipping mint tea in the ebbing heat of the day,
I recollect how we stumbled onto a raccoon
squashed between boards leaning against a fence,
tadpoles wriggling at the edge of a pond.
On the living-room table, thirty-six peonies
in a vase dry and become crepe-paper light
to touch. Yesterday you watered blue chamisa
along the county road, while I watered desert grass
under the willow. I recollect opening a brown,
humid box and, stunned, lifted a handful
of morels, inhaling the black aroma of earth.
What is it we give each other—gold, shark's fin—
other than a renewed sense of the miraculous?
Nanao watched a blip on the radar screen; later,
when he saw the flash, he thought Mt. Fuji
had erupted in a burst of light. Sipping mint tea
on the longest day of the year, I sense how
the balance of a life sways, and a petal may tip it.

7

A steady evening with a first-quarter moon;
numerous craters along the terminator are razor sharp;

I observe the ghostly bluish glow of earthshine
and feel how the moon has no permanent dark side.

A horse neighs by the barbed-wire fence;
we trudge into a wet field, carrying, from under the portal,

a bee's nest in a basket, place it in a nook
of a silver poplar. Will any bees hatch in spring?

I notice thorns on the bare branches of Russian olives;
you spot coyote scat before the V-shaped gate.

We walk to where the Pojoaque and Nambé flow together—
I am amazed at how we blossom into each other.

I hear the occasional drone of cars on Highway 285,
hear how the living expire into smoke

and the dead inflame the minds of the living.
When I exhale against a cold window, I see

the ever-shifting line along the terminator;
and, as the shadow cast by the rim of Theophilus

slips across the crater's floor, I feel light
surge into a honeycomb gold—it all goes and comes at once.

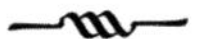

Ox-Head Dot

Ox-head dot, wasp waist, mouse tail,
bamboo section, water-caltrop, broken branch,
stork leg, a pole for carrying fuel:
these are the eight defects when a beginning
calligrapher has no bone to a stroke.

I have no names for what can go wrong:
peeling carrots, a woman collapses
when a tumor in her kidney ruptures;
bronze slivers from a gimbal nut
jam the horizontal stabilizer to a jet,

make it plunge into the Pacific Ocean;
"Hyena!" a man shouts into the darkness
and slams shut the door. Stunned, I hear
a scratching, know that I must fumble,
blunder, mistake, fail; yet, sometimes

in the darkest space is a white fleck,
ox-head dot; and when I pass through,
it's a spurt of match into flame,
glowing moths loosed into air, air
rippling, roiling the surface of the world.

Syzygy

I notice headlights out the living-room window
then catch the bass in a pickup as it drives by.
I am shocked to learn that doctors collected
the urine of menopausal nuns in Italy to extract
gonadotropins. And is that what one draws,
in infinitesimal dose, out of a vial?
I remember a steel-wool splinter in my finger
and how difficult it was to discern, extract
under a magnifying glass; yet—blue mold,
apple dropping from branch—it is hard to see
up close when, at the periphery, the unexpected
easily catches the eye. Last Thursday night,
we looked through binoculars at the full moon,
watched it darken and darken until, eclipsed,
it glowed ferrous-red. By firelight, we glowed;
my fingertips flared when I rubbed your shoulders,
softly bit your ear. The mind is a tuning fork
that we strike, and, struck, in the syzygy
of a moment, we find the skewed, tangled
passions of a day begin to straighten, align, hum.

La Bajada

Driving north before Cochiti exit, he visualizes
a bleeding anthropologist pulled from a wrecked car

but encounters only starlight and wind. Tonight
cars glide past him at eighty. Marine biologists

believed the coelacanth was extinct until a fisherman
off Madagascar pulled one up in a net. After 400,000

photographs in a bubble chamber, technicians had no track
of omega minus and wanted to quit. Sometimes luck

and sometimes perseverance. In the morning he stirred
to agapanthus odor, felt presence and absence

resemble an asymptotic line and curve that squeeze
closer and closer but do not touch. He glances up

at Cassiopeia arcing toward the north-northwest,
wonders if mosquito eggs in the pond are about to hatch,

sees her trim red and orange ranunculus on the counter.
And as he pushes on the gas and begins to ascend

La Bajada, water runs in the acequia
behind the kitchen porch for the first time this year.

Spring Smoke

The minutes ooze into a honeycomb gold.
He reads in a recently discovered notebook

that in 1941 his grandfather refused
to collaborate with the puppet government

and was kidnapped in Shanghai, held
in a smoky loft where he breathed

through a hole in the roof while his captors
unloaded, reloaded revolvers, played

mah-jongg. He pauses to adjust the light,
wonders if the wasp nest lodged on a beam

in the shed is growing. His grandfather
describes a woman who refused to divulge

where her husband was until they poured
scalding tea down her throat and crushed

her right hand in a vise. He glances up
but cannot discern stars through the skylight.

He senses smoky gold notes rising
out of a horn and knows how easy it is

to scald, blister, burst. This morning
when he drew back a wood slat

to swing the gate, he glimpsed a young
pear tree blossoming in the driveway.

Haircutting

She snips his hair with new scissors.
He ponders rain on the skylight, x^x;

his father sent him an elephant tusk
carved into a village with lotus ponds

and waterfalls. His son, asleep, left
on the kitchen table in an unwaxed bag

clusters of chanterelles. Who probes
for ice crystals below the moon's surface?

He recalls a physicist who loved to raft
the Taos Box, complained of recurring

headaches, had a stroke, died. She is
wearing a string of graduated pearls

with a jade clasp. He puts his hands
on her hips, savors unbuttoning her blouse.

When a letter from Peter arrived today,
he slit it open: violin, *jarana,* harp music

from La Sierra de Zongolica spilled out.
In the aftermath of a miscarriage,

she loops back to a moonrise over White Sands,
to a skunkbush sumac in a transverse dune.

Lobed Bowl with Black Glaze and White Scalloped Rim

Turning from the obituary page,
he hears a screw tighten,
recalls a dead sparrow on a greenhouse floor.

The mind can be dipped in a vat
when you slice an eggplant, sharpen a pencil,
shave. He woke slowly as light

sank through the skylight, brightening
the bedroom. He recalls running
his tongue from her breast to her armpit

as she shivered with pleasure.
An elder holds an eagle feather,
wafts cedar smoke, taps a woman

on her shoulders. He wants a mind
as pure as a ten-lobed bowl
with black glaze and white scalloped rim.

A broad-tailed hummingbird whirs in the air—
and in a dewdrop on a mimosa leaf
is the day's angular momentum.

Quipu

1

I try to see a bald eagle nest in a Douglas fir
but catch my sleeve on thorns, notice blackberries,

hear large wings splashing water in a lagoon.
I glimpse a heron perched on a post above a tidal flat,

remember red elderberries arcing along a path
where you catch and release a newt among ferns.

And as a doe slips across the road behind us,
we zigzag when we encounter a point of resistance,

zigzag as if we describe the edge of an immense leaf,
as if we plumb a jagged coastline where tides

wash and renew the mind. I stare at abalone eyes,
am startled at how soft a sunflower star is to touch,

how sticky a tentacle of an anemone is to finger.
When we walk barefoot in sand, I sway

to the motion of waves, mark bits of crabs
washed to shore, see—in an instant a dog wrenches

a leash around the hand of a woman, shatters bones—
ensuing loss salamanders the body, lagoons the mind.

2

Here a red horse leaned over a barbed-wire fence
and uprooted a row of corn; here chile plants
rotted after a thunderstorm; here the force of rain
exposed carrot seeds and washed almost all away;
but here two kinds of eggplants flower in a row;

here peas, cucumbers, bell peppers, eggplants,
tomatoes, melons, corn. Is this wave of flowering
the arc of loss? She closes her eyes and aches:
in a white room, the ultrasound picks up yolk sac
and curled embryo: inside the space of a pea,

a head, mouth, neural tube, brain stem, eyes;
but it does not pulse or flicker with a heartbeat.
Across the room, they reach out, but to what?
The room darkens as the screen ionizes, glows.
He visualizes a series of photographic still lifes:

polished tin doorknob against a black background,
whale vertebra seen from afar against a black background,
nineteen stacked pancakes against a black background,
cluster of hazelnuts up close against a black background;
and suddenly when he opens his eyes, he cannot hear.

3

Who touched a quipu and made it explode into dust?

What blooms as briefly as scarlet gaura in sandy soil?

How incandescent is a grief?

Did spun wool delineating the corn of the Incas obliterate in a second?

What incipient white fades into pink?

Did the knots of her loves jaguar in an instant?

What is the tensile strength of a joy?

Who observed a great horned owl regurgitate bones into the arroyo?

What hides in the wave of a day?

A single blue unknotted cord—what does it mean?

How can the mind ply the forms of desire?

From south to north, east to west: which length is greater?

When is a koan not a koan?

Who can unravel the spin of an elegy and counterspin it into an ode?

Who whispered, "as is"?

Where is a passion that orchids the body?

Whose carded cotton fibers are these?

4

7:14: red numbers on the clock incarnadine the time;
he stares at the maroon jar of a kerosene lamp,
the carmine batik hanging under a skylight.

And when he drives home, the red at the Stop sign
is the bright red blood on a sheet;
yet candles in the living room conjure bliss.

He has the urge to stroll down to a spring-fed pond
where he sits on a rusted bench, stares into water;
tiny fish dart near; a green frog lifts its head;

then a vermilion dragonfly hovers near irises,
zigzags back and forth as it weaves an invisible web.
He guesses it eats mosquitoes and midges, though

he can only catch sunlight glint off its wings.
The mind zigzags back—swimming in a tidal pond,
they brushed jellyfish with their arms and legs—

loops a red cord that records loss and loss.
When he trudges back and closes his eyes,
he is startled by a cricket chirping in the fireplace.

5

When he opened the book to the page with *quipu,*
he glimpsed, through the underside of the sheet,

the image of a quince. Sometimes the thing you want
bleeds *in* the light. When yellow leaves dropped

off the cottonwood, he spotted, up high, a large nest
and a magpie hopping from branch to branch.

When he stubbed his toe in the dark, he flashed
on how he dug his first matsutake out of the dirt,

fingered brown scales on the cap and stalk.
As he stares into her eyes, she relates how

two men, rescued in the Andes, suffered frostbite:
one had his arms and legs amputated but is

moving with artificial limbs, while the other,
who tried to hold on to his extremities, suffers

in a wheelchair. When he says, "I don't want
to become *that,*" the *no* smears fingerprints on glass.

And he sees a man splashed with blood and scales
stand hip deep in halibut, cleaning them off.

6

Who has heard a flute carved from the wing bone of a crane?

they hung tomato plants upside down in the kitchen;

a dyer poured fermented piss into the dye bath;

explosion of egg and sperm;

a hummingbird nest tucked in some branches
tucked in his mind;

she groaned when he yanked her hair back;

inside the space of a pea,
beginningless beginning and endless end;

he diverts water from the acequia, irrigates slender peach trees;

when he pulled the skeins up,
they gasped when they turned blue in the air;

they folded an ultrasound image inside a red envelope with a white crane,
prayed, set it on fire;

he wove a blue jaguar;

plucking ripened tomatoes, she grazed shriveled leaves;

"All men are mortal";

they prayed to the sun, burned the blue jaguar at noon;

conception: 186,000 miles per second;

186,000 miles per second;

who has heard a flute carved from the wing bone of a crane?

7

Crows pick at a dead buffalo along the curve
of the river, as Raz trots up with a cow hoof

in his mouth. As: to the same degree or amount;
for instance; when considered in a specified

form or relation; in or to the same degree
in which; as if; in the way or manner that;

in accordance with what or the way in which;
while, when; regardless of the degree to which;

for the reason that; that the result is.
As in a quipu where colored, knotted strings

hang off a primary cord—or as a series
of acequias off the Pojoaque River drop water

into fields—the mind ties knots, and I
follow a series of short strings to a loose end—

stepping barefoot in white sand, rolling
down a dune, white flecks on our lips,

on our eyelids, sitting in a warm dune
as a gibbous moon lifts against the sky's pelagic,

with the shadows of fourwing saltbushes,
the scent of hoary rosemarymint in the air.

8

I close my eyes—fishhooks and nylon threads
against a black background, cuttlefish
from above against a black background,

blowfish up close against a black background.
The seconds are as hushed as the morning
after steady snowfall when the power is out,

the rooms cold. At one, a snow-heavy branch
snapped the power line; the loose end flailed
clusters of orange sparks. A woman swept

a walkway, missed a porch step, fell forward,
bruised her face, broke both elbows; yet
the body quickens in the precarious splendor

that *it would not be better if things happened*
to men just as they wish, that—moonglow,
sunrise—the day—scales of carp in frost on glass—

scalds and stuns. In 1,369 days, we've set
eagle to eagle feather and formed a nest
where—fishhook joy—the mind is new each day.

9

We bend to enter a cave at Tsankawi, inadvertently
stir some tufa dust, notice it catches a beam

of sunlight. The beam enters a ceiling shaft
at winter solstice noon and forms, on a plastered wall,

a slash, then a small circle of intense light
before it disappears. And when we leave,

you sizzle with the vanished point of light.
I sizzle when I remember how we first kissed,

when I ran my hands along your shoulders,
when you brushed lashes on my neck. And as flying

geese cast shadows on water, and water reflects
the light, a joy stretches and stretches

into the infinite. I recall when we knocked at
our neighbors' door to drop off a gift, how

they didn't hear us as they were staring out
at the feeder counting birds—bushtit, sapsucker,

nuthatch, woodpecker—as we counted the blessing
of seconds where heat shimmered and vanished into air.

Aqueous Gold

1

At six a.m., the Big Dipper has swung overhead;
in an hour you will look up to rose-tinged
cirrus clouds. When I shut my eyes, waves
unfurl; I rouse to cries of birds before
sunrise, recall the imprint of our bodies
in white sand; from the beach, water deepens
into teal blue in no time. Aqueous gold
ripples on the surfaces of waves, but when
you reach for it there, it is here, and
when you reach for it here, it vanishes.
The mind craves to make something perdurable
out of something as tenuous as candlelight,
something that becomes more and more itself
through vicissitude. When a selenographer
plots the moon's seas, does he inscribe
a memory that can batter as well as renew?
We kindle into flame a firelight by which
we incandesce more and more of ourselves.
Inscribed in the motion of birth and death,
we poise, savor the resistance to move too soon.

2

In the impoverishment of memory, you listen
to a cricket crawl in a pipe below the sink
but cannot see it, finger a cracked vase,
yet treasure its sliver of death. When you
reach out to touch a woman on her deathbed,
the flush of her skin is no longer a surprise:
eyes closed, absorbing oxygen through a tube,
she will never hate, love, sing, connive,
speak, stir again. In a barrio apartment,
you pull on a light: cockroaches flick
their forelegs and snap flat their forewings.
You listen to the drone of a refrigerator,
drips from faucets. In a Ketchikan bar,
a man trembles and recounts how a bear swiped
his right eye, how the eye ran like raw egg,
though you surmise he moves from bar to bar
to repeat his pain. You step out into drizzle:
the snow line has dropped to eighty feet
above the docks. Thoughts inch through
memory the way maggots inch through a cèpe.

3

A candle undulates on the mantel; at the end
of winter, water in the pond is clear with
twig and leaf debris clumped at the bottom.
They yearn for an instant that clears the mind;
in the warm yellow light at their fingertips,
they sense what dies is cast into the molten
form of the moment, as prayers are tossed
into the molten cast of a bell: *yellow,*
this, sun, wet, shudder, shriek, torque, be.
Though a potter can remove with tongs a molten
bowl from a kiln, plunge it in water,
they have nothing but a snake of words
to prove this moment when a chrysanthemum
unfolds in steaming broth in a black bowl;
when it heats, warms their hands; when they
recognize a pale green leaf is beginning
to flare out; apple tree beginning to bud;
when a sliver of moon begins to widen;
when they quiver and end this stillness,
begin to stretch into another glistening stillness.

4

Tying a balloon to the zoo's iron gate, he catches
the blink of a cashier before she rings
up another fee, hungers for the moment a turtle
slips into water. Inside, he pauses at a tank,
views nothing, puts his hands on glass; at once
a phalanx of piranhas veer and repel light.
He studies their glistening jaws, eyes, incisors,
turns to a peacock pacing back and forth
on the floorboards, scarlet ibises with folded wings.
A single loss can ravel the mind with grief
and—meteor shower—hours days minutes seconds—
make us reach for white narcissi by the window
at sunrise. In the park, crimson and orange
oak leaves burn into transparency: is a moment
of death a seed? A friend once ignited fireworks
over a dry lake to tremble what expires
and what persists: streaming red gossamers,
yellow showers, violet chrysanthemums arcing
into gold into black air. Bending to tie a shoelace,
he confronts pocked craters in the irregular asphalt.

5

In a few minutes the sky lightens so that
branches of the willow flare to the very twig.
The hiss when a molten bowl is plunged into water
is also the hiss when you ladle water onto rocks
in the sauna. It is not in the hoofprints of zebras
or in the shadows of oryxes, but in the scent
of a lynx by a goose pen. The warmth and aroma of wax
in this flickering room is not to be inscribed
on papyrus wrapped around a corpse, nor is it
currency to be burned into the next fearless world.
It is when we true ourselves to the consequence
that we find the yellow lightning of our kiss.
Though we sit inscribed in a circle, we twist
and smell a wild fennel stalk in our hands.
Moose calves with dangling wet umbilical cords
struggle to keep up with their long-legged fast-
moving mothers. As we go up a series of wooden steps,
we gaze down, and, as large multicolored koi
leisurely swim in the pool below, one koi
flaps and shivers gold flecks onto the surface.

6

Clusters of wild irises shrivel in the field.
He tries to slide the ring off his mother's
finger, but rigor mortis has set in; he soaps
her finger, swivels the ring, yanks it off.
I catch the motion with which a man tosses
water from a brush onto a setting cement curb,
while another trowels the cement to an olive shine.
We did not notice when rain stopped striking
the skylight but glance up at a crack that
runs through the glass. "Yum!" a twenty-year-old
exclaims, pours milk onto cornflakes, snot
smeared across his face, while his stepmother
convulses, breaks into sobs. We place hoops
around peonies so that growing buds will not bend
stalks to the ground. I search for swaying lines
of ants, but nothing is there; I survey irregular
white trunks of aspens, but nothing is there.
As *that* swivels into *this,* I thread a tiny
screw to fasten the bracelet around your wrist;
you pull back a wooden slat to open the gate.

Solstice Quipu

Hong Kong 87, New York 84;
he studies isobars on the weather map;

ashes accumulate at the tip of an incense stick;

mosquitoes are hatching near the Arctic Circle;

300,000 acres in Arizona scorched or aflame;

the aroma of *genmai* tea from a teapot with no lid;

where is the Long March now?
And Lin Biao—so what if
he salivated behind a one-way mirror at naked women?

lobstermen color code their buoys;

string sandals number knotted mine the gold of the output of s on—
though things are not yet in their places,
the truth sears his fingertips:

the output of gold mines,
the number of sandals knotted on string;

orange globe of sun refracted through haze;

a two-year-old gasps at hummingbirds lying on a porch;

he notes a torn screen, nods
male and *female, black-chinned;*
spells the iridescent gorget of spring.

Inflorescence

1

Go sway on a suspension bridge over a gorge;
you do not ponder the beauty of an azure
lotus-shaped wine-warming bowl with five
spurs the size of sesame seeds at the base,
but, instead, inhale the cool mist sliding
over pines, making the white boulders below
disappear and reappear. This is how you
become absent to pancakes smoking on a griddle—
pricked once in thought, you are pinned,
singed back to the watery splendor of the hour:
wisteria leaves thin to transparency on the porch;
a girl relaxes on horseback in the field
while sunlight stipples her neck. You smile,
catch the aroma of pumpkin seeds in the oven,
exult at the airy, spun filaments of clouds.
Before there was above and below, who was there
to query? One marks a bloody trail in water
from a harpooned narwhal, dreams of clustered
igloos lit by seal oil. You flicker, nod:
what one has is steeped in oil, wicked into flame.

2

Whisked back and forth,
a fly
drops on water;

> a floating narwhal
> resembles a human corpse;

screwdrivers, pliers, CDs,
a duct-taped taillight
strewn in the grass;

> running my tongue
> along your nape;

singed by
apple leaves
on the windshield;

> smooth black stones
> in a glass bowl;

where the mind
that is
no-mind is;

> fingertips
> on a frosted pane.

3

A shrinking loop becomes a noose: at the airport
a Choctaw writer scrawls a few words to his wife,
creases the paper, fires a slug into his chest.
A woman smokes, ruminates on a blank canvas
she does not yet know will remain blank.
I push hoops into the dirt, prop up a few
tomato branches: a single Black Krim has reseeded
from last summer. I uproot some weeds, toss them,
but, in thought, recoil from flies on a squirrel;
raise a lid to a plastic barrel: find hamburger
wrappers, stomped soda cans, irregular bits
of white glass near where I vacuum my car.
As a red snake snags its epidermis, the mind snags,
molts from inside out. Although sand plunges
in an hourglass—soon the last white particles
will vanish from the top—I ache for a second,
sulfur butterfly pinned over black paper, to stop:
but, eelgrass in tidal water, I catch the scent
of tomato leaves on my hands, swing palms near
a horse's head: flies flit and land, flit and reland.

4

Incise the beginning and end to all motion;

q w e r t y u i o p, in a line above your fingertips;

align river stones for a walkway;

halt at clusters of notes from swinging copper-green wind chimes;

shovel twigs and beer cans out of a ditch;

this wave of pollen light on your face is the end of summer;

rub Maximilian sunflower petals with your hands;

sniff red silk pine-bark patterned gauze unearthed out of a tomb;

splay juniper with an ax;

water brims her eyes when you stroke her wrist;

a *Bombyx mori* consumes mulberry leaves for seven days;

ponder a missing shade of blue;

sweat when you eat that Chimayó chile stuffed with lamb;

graze patches of faint aquamarine paint on a bathroom door;

revolve a polygon inside a circle;

squint up at a magpie nest in the cottonwood branches;

survey a skater's mark left on the ice in executing a half-turn;

inscribe the beginning and end to all motion.

5

In the zero sunlight a man at a traffic light
waving today's newspaper becomes a man
who, wiping windshields at night in a drizzle
as cars come off the Brooklyn Bridge,
opens his hands. Behind your parked car,
you stoop to peruse a speckled brown egg
on the gravel, glance up to sight a ring-tailed
lemur on a branch. Though no red-winged
blackbirds nest in the cattails this summer,
though someone has tried to drain the pond
into a nearby acequia, there is nothing
to drain, and you nod, curse, laugh—
you have nothing, everything in mind.
When I run my fingers between your fingers,
when we wet river wet through white Embudo water,
the hush is a shocked stillness: a black
bug stretches the skin of water and circles out.
As moonlight slants through the screen door,
I mark the span of our lives suspended
over the undulating scritch scratch of crickets.

6

I sip warm wine out of a sky-blue bowl
flecked with agate crystals in the glaze,

press my eyes, squint at walruses on an ice floe.
When you step on stones in plover formation

and enter a tea garden—shift the rhythm
of your body, mind; admire the slender

splayed arc of branches, singed maple leaves
scattered on gravel—you arrive at the cusp

where you push open a blue-planked door,
inhale the aroma of a miniature calla lily

in an oblong vase, bend over a brass trash can
to find a cluster of ants that must have

dropped from the ceiling and, disoriented, died.
And as the configuration at dusk of flaring

willow leaves on the skylight becomes minnows
in water, what is above becomes what is below.

And what appears up close to be a line
becomes, by air, the arc of a circle.

7

A woman and an instructor skydive over an island;
their parachutes fail, and they plunge into a yard,
barely missing someone snipping morning glories.
How long did they free-fall before they knew
the end? We stare at Dungeness crab shells strewn
across the table, pull cupcakes out of the oven,
and, smoothing icing on them to the rhythm of
African drumming, sizzle along a cusp of dream.
Who knows what the Coal Sack in the Milky Way is?
Who cares that the Eta Carinae Nebula is about
9,000 light-years distant? A moment in the body
is beauty's memento mori: when I rake gravel in
a courtyard, or sweep apricot leaves off a deck,
I know an inexorable inflorescence in May sunshine;
watch a man compose a flower arrangement
in Tokyo using polychrome Acoma pots. And as
a narwhal tusk pokes out of a hole in the ice,
as a thumbprint momentarily forms in thawing frost
on a pane, we heat a precarious splendor,
inscribe the end and beginning to all motion.

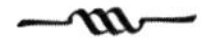

Oracle-Bone Script

In oracle-bone script, the character for *attunement*
is a series of bamboo pipes tied together with string;
if only I had the words to make things that accord
in tone vibrate together. Sunlight streams between slats
of a fence onto the ground. I gaze across the field;
skunks have slipped into the neighbor's garden
and ravaged corn. At the mouth of an arroyo, someone
has drained engine oil into the sand, thrown quart
containers into the brush. "Goddamn," I whisper,
bending to pick cherry tomatoes, discover a large
grasshopper sunning on a branch. I imagine holding
a set of black-lacquered panpipes, blowing on them
for the first time in two thousand years. In the wobbly
beginning is a swish, then water trembling through bamboo,
tossed gravel, a dog's bark, throats slit, sleet,
footsteps, love-cries. I start as notes reverberate
in air; frost has shriveled the leaves into black bits.

The Welt

He longs for a day marked like a Song tea bowl
with indented lip and hare's-fur markings.

Yesterday they skirted two decomposing lambs
at the entrance to the big arroyo, covered

their mouths as they approached from downwind.
During firing, gravity pulls iron-oxide

slip down to form a hare's-fur pattern
on the glaze surface. They gagged at the stench,

saw pink plastic twine around the neck
of the mangled one by the post—he only wanted

to view it once. They moved on to the low-
voltage fence, looked for bison but saw none,

tried to spark the fence with a thrown stick.
He likes the plum blossom heat when

their bodies sway and thrash. They returned
along a smaller arroyo. In the aftermath,

cool to touch, a ghost of the body's heat.
In the morning they woke to sunburn on their necks.

In the Living Room

I turn this green hexagonal tile with
a blue dragonfly, but what is it I am turning?
The vertical scroll on the far wall

has seven characters that roughly translate,
"The sun's reflection on the Yangtze River
is ten thousand miles of gold." A Japanese

calligrapher drew these Chinese characters
in the 1890s, but who knows the circumstances
of the event? I graze the crackled paper,

recognize a moment ready to scrape into flame;
gaze at ceiling beams from Las Trampas,
at Peñasco floorboards softened with lye.

Along the wall on a pedestal, a gold-leafed
male and female figure join in sexual embrace.
Hours earlier, my hands held your hips,

your breasts brushed my chest. I close
my eyes, feel how in the circumference
of a circle the beginning and end have no end.

Acanthus

When you shut your eyes, you find a string
of mackerel tied by their tails over and across
the sloping street; pour water into raki
and watch it cloud into "lion's milk";
nibble smoked aubergine with yogurt;
point to red mullet on a platter of fish.
You catch the sound of dripping water,
squat to be near to the upside-down Medusa
head at the column base in a cistern:
a drop of water splashes your forehead.
You note carved acanthus leaves, then
eighteen women in singular postures
of mourning along the sides of a sarcophagus;
turn, at a noise, to bright lights:
eighteen men and women in security shirts
swarm through the covered street,
search for heroin. You smell saffron,
cardamom, frankincense, cinnamon, ginger,
galingale, thyme, star anise, fennel:
open your eyes to leeches in a jar
half-filled with water—green powdered henna
in a box alongside white mulberries.
The bells around the necks of goats clink;
you run your fingers along the fragments
of terra-cotta pots built into the stone
walls of houses; blink at the beggar
whose foot has swollen to the size
of his head; stagger up to Athena's temple
by moonlight; sit on a broken column,
gaze out across the gulf to Lesbos,
where lights glimmer along the curve
of a bay. In waxing moonlight, the water
is riffled, argentine, into wide patches.
You ache at how passion is a tangle
of silk in your hands, shut your eyes,
unstring the silk in one continuous thread.

The Thermos

Poppy seeds from a North Bennington garden
rest in white envelopes on a *granero*
in Jacona—to travel far is to return.
I am not thinking about the glitter of snow

on top of Popocatepetl, but how beauty
that is not beauty requires distance.
I recall the emerald gleam of glacier ice,
bald eagles perched at the tip of Homer Spit.

When I brought home that turtle-shaped
sandbox, we placed a giraffe, lion, tiger
at the edge. Sarah was happy to tilt sand
from her yellow shovel into a blue pail.

I scooped sand into a funnel and watched it
drain into the box. I do not know how
an amethyst crystal begins to take shape;
I do not know the nanoproperties of

silica or the origin of light, but I
know the moment a seed bursts its husk.
At work I spill tea out of a thermos,
smell your hair and how we quicken each other.

Ice Line

No one has slowed down
and battered mailboxes
at the junction;
at two a.m. a cricket
periodically chirps
in a corner of the bathroom;
earlier in the day,
a horsefly bit
into Sarah's back,
and her cry
ululated in the air;
later she peered at rain
in a Hiroshige print
where men in bamboo hats
leaned into
the relentless, slanting drizzle
then pointed up at the skylight
where raindrops
were pooled on glass;
each night is a brimming
pool of light,
and the contours are as
intricate and shifting as
the ice line around Antarctica.

The Chromatics of Dawn

Navel oranges ripen on branches near the steps
to a porch. He recalls zigzagging along a path

marked by white stones through a lava flow
to a beach where violet morning glories flared.

Up the coast he once peered into the water
but could not discern the underwater shrine

frequented by black-tipped reef sharks.
He tries to delineate the sheen of rolling waves,

chromatics to this hour when light pales
the unfolded paper shades to the south-

facing French doors. Last Wednesday they rolled
architectural plans, along with sun-bleached

red paper inscribed with gold characters,
and torched them in the hearth. As they remodel,

they ponder how a floor of repeating strips
of bolted oak and cement can be replicated;

but, at his fingertips, he finds nothing
can be replicated: neither the hair in her hairbrush

nor the hole in his sock, neither the hue
of sunrise nor waves of opalescent spring sleet.

Thermodynamics

He tips hot water into a cup, stirs the powdered
Lingzhi mushroom, hands it to you. You observe
black specks swirling in the inky tonic: sip,
shudder, sip. It is supposed to treat neurasthenia,
dizziness, insomnia, high serum cholesterol,
coronary disease, rhinitis, asthma, duodenal ulcers,
boost the immune system. You scan the room,
catch crescendos and decrescendos to the flute
music on the stand, pick out the first character,
Spring, written in official script on a scroll—
Warring States bronze mirrors lined up on stands.
You pick up the last strands of glistening jellyfish,
note speckled tracks of grease on the platter,
feel as if you are jostled in a small airplane
as it descends into cumulus clouds. In Beijing
a couple wanted to thank him for arranging
financial sponsorship of their son in America;
under the table, she rubbed her leg against his
and whispered she had tomorrow off from work;
but *tomorrow, lust, betrayal, delight, yesterday,*
ardor, scorn, forgiveness are music from empty holes,
and you wonder if the haphazard course of a life
follows a fundamental equation in thermodynamics.
He pulls Styrofoam out of a box and reveals
a two-foot-high human figure from the tomb of
the Third Han Emperor; the face and trunk are intact,
though arms and hands are gone. He bequeaths
it to you, though requests that you pass it on
someday to a museum. You nod, sip the cool tonic,
down a few last black specks at the bottom of the cup.

X and O

Someone flips a lit match off the road
near a cluster of cattails, takes
another swig of beer, presses on the gas;
the match is not specifically aimed
at you: you just happen to be there—
at a Stop sign, in a parking lot,
on a ferry, at a terminal; as a lens
narrows sunlight to a point which blackens
into flame, go ahead, zero in, try
to x out a ball of jasmine sprig
that unfurls in boiling water, x out
a red-tailed hawk shifting on a cottonwood
branch at dusk, x out coyotes yipping
as they roam by new moonlight up the road,
x out the dissolving suture threads
in your mouth, x out a dog's bark,
a baby magpie fallen from a nest
wandering on gravel, x out a flicker
feather in the mud; you can't x out
diarrhea, x out a barn erupted into flames,
x out firefighters lined up in trucks
along Russian olives, x out the charred
grass and stubs of fence posts, x out
a pang, place of birth or time of death,
x out, at an intersection of abscissa
and ordinate, dark matter that warps
space and time; you can't x out a cloud,
so make a lens of it the next time
you chop cilantro at a counter, the next
time you push through a turnstile.

The Angle of Reflection Equals the Angle of Incidence

Take that and that and that and that and—

a kid repeatedly kicks a dog near where
raw sewage gurgles onto sand at low tide,

Málaga, 1971. A man rummaging in a ravine
of trash is scrunched by a bulldozer.

If only I had q or r or s dissolves

into floaters in her eyes. Simmer. Scattered
ashes on blue-black Atlantic waves bob

and tinkle in the rippling tide of morning.
How quickly at dawn one makes out power lines,

cloud, fence, blue awning, orchard, plank

over ditch, but twisting chimney smoke
incites one to mark white apple blossoms

by a low gate, whale bones in a backyard,
chile roasting in a parking lot, or the memory

of wrapping an exposed pipe, the sizzle

when our tongues meet. When dead leaves
flowed downstream and encountered a sword,

they were razored in two. One, two,
four, eight: surmise a molten sword has

32,768 pounded layers before a final hissing.

Who believes what is written will never perish?
In 1258 Mongols hurled books into the Tigris

River and dyed the water black with ink.
Although a first record tabulating sheep and goats

has disappeared from a museum, the notation is

never expunged but is always renewed, amplified,
transmogrified. When a woman gives you a sheet

of handmade magnolia paper with mica flecks,
you lift it up to light, a milk snake's

translucent skin slides off. Though a strand

of silk unfurls to become a kilometer long,
tracks are not the only incubator of dreams.

So you missed the Eta Aquarid meteor shower,
or last week's total lunar eclipse. When you

sweep cobwebs out of the fireplace, sneeze,

scrutinize the veins of a peony leaf, you mark
the vertiginous moment of your beginning,

catch and release what you cannot hold,
smell kumquats in a glass bowl, stare down

at hundreds of red ants simultaneously fanning

out and converging at a point of emergence.
After a motorcycle blares past the north window,

the silence accretes: a rose quartz crystal
in the night. I garner the aroma of seared

scallops on a bamboo skewer; the ashes of

the woman who savored them scattered on waves.
Can watermelon seeds germinate in this moonlight?

The hairbrush, soap, thermometer by the sink
form a moment's figure that dissolves

as easily as an untied knot. A plumber fluent

in Sanskrit corrects my pronunciation of *dhyāna*
while he replaces a chrome faucet fixture.

I pore over a cross-sectional drawing of a plum;
is an infinitesimal seed at the cross-

sectional center of the cosmos? Though a vibrating

crystal can measure increments, time itself
is a black thread. I arrive at a vernal cusp:

the murmur you make on the tide of sleep;
the sleigh-like sounds when we caress.

Who waits and waits at a feeder for yesterday's

indigo bunting to arrive? A woman curls grape
roots into a sculpture, mentions her husband

died three years ago. We do not shut the eyelids
of the deceased, nor are we tied in quinine-soaked

sheets for delineating the truth. Once you begin,

the branching is endless: miller moths spiral
against a screened porch; we apprehend the shadows

of leaves on leaves, regard a goldfinch
feeding outside a window, a sparrow that keeps

flinging itself into glass. When a minute stillness

is sifted out of the noise, a whirlpool becomes
a spiral galaxy. When I run my tongue along

your clavicle, we dig clamshells out of the sand,
net red crabs at low tide. In the wren song

of brief rain, what matters is that we instill

the darkness with jade, live clear-eyed incising
a peony-blossoming dawn. And as someone trans-

plants bell peppers and onions into a garden,
leaves on a stream approach another sword

but, when they are about to touch, are repelled.

Quinoa simmers in a pot; the aroma of cilantro
on swordfish; the cusp of spring when you

lean your head on my shoulder. Orange crocuses
in the backyard form a linc. *Once* is a scorched site;

we stoop in the grass, finger twelve keys with

interconnected rings on a swiveling yin-yang coin,
dangle them from the gate, but no one claims them.

Our meandering intersects with the vanished
in ways we do not comprehend: as a primary cord

may consist of two-ply two-color s-plied cords

joined by z-spiraling single-colored simple cord:
I note the creaking cottonwood branch overhead;

moon below Venus in morning twilight; in our arms
one season effloresces into another into another.

The polar ice caps of Mars advance and retreat

with their seasons. Sometimes in gazing afar,
we locate ourselves. We were swimming in a river

below a sloping waterfall; I recalled wandering
away from the main peony garden and pausing

in front of blue poppies. To recollect is to

renew, invigorate, regenerate. A papyrus shoot
spikes out of a copper tub. *Hang glider, sludge,*

pixel, rhinoceros horn, comb, columbarium,
wide-angle, spastic, Leica lens, pincushion—

these have no through-line except that all

things becoming and unbecoming become part
of the floe. When I stare at a photograph

and count two hundred sixty-five hazelnuts,
examine the irregular cracks in their shells,

I recognize fractures in turtle plastrons,

glimpse the divinatory nature of language.
And as a lantern undulating on the surface

of a black pool is not the lantern itself,
so these synapsed words are not the things

themselves but, sizzling, point the way.

Earthstar

Opening the screen door, you find a fat spider
poised at the threshold. When I swat it,

hundreds of tiny crawling spiders burst out.
What space in the mind bursts into waves

of wriggling light? As we round a bend,
a gibbous moon burnishes lava rocks and waves.

A wild boar steps into the road, and, around
another bend, a mongoose darts across our headlights.

As spokes to a hub, the very far converges
to the very near. A row of Siberian irises

buds and blooms in the yard behind our bedroom.
A moth flutters against a screen and sets

off a light. I had no idea carded wool spun
into yarn could be dipped and oxidized into bliss.

Once, hunting for chanterelles in a meadow,
I flushed quail out of the brush. Now

you step on an unexpected earthstar, and it
bursts in a cloud of brown spores into June light.

Didyma

1

Disoriented, a woman wanders in the riverbed
east then west then east, asks us how to get
to County Road 101G. We stare at vertebrae
and long bones that protrude out of her plastic bag,
discern how one day the scavenger will become
the scavenged. At thirteen you dipped leaves
into melted wax in an aluminum pan on a stove,
had an inkling that in order to seal the shapes
you had to asphyxiate the leaves. And as
the area of your knowledge grew, the circumference
of your ignorance was always increased. You had
no idea you would live to recall so many deaths,
that they would become spots along a Pacific
coastline where you would come to gather salt.
You yearn for the ocean spray to quicken your eyes,
yearn for the woman you love to sway and rock.
When she sways and rocks, you sway and rock;
when you sway and rock, she sways and rocks;
when you convulse together, it is not hallucinatory
but a splendor that scavenges days and nights.

2

The shortest distance between two points is a straight line;

"Slob!"

red salamanders spawned in the Tesuque River;

an ocelot placed a paw on his chest while he slept;

he slapped a mosquito between his hands;

the position of beads on the abacus represented nyctalopia;

asphyxiated in a hotel room;

water in the black rubber bucket froze and never thawed;

red-winged blackbirds congregate in the cattails;

when he closed his eyes, she was there;
when he opened his eyes, she was there;

was afraid to cut the deck;

mosquito larvae quiver the water in the barrel;

rubbed her nipples;

sighted a rhinoceros in the crosshairs and went blind;

rearranged a tangram into the shape of a butterfly;

when he took off his glasses,
oncoming headlights became volvox floating on black water;

slashed the waves with ten thousand whips;

sunlight erased blue thumbprints but left the graphite lines unscathed;

"The earth rests upon water."

3

What can be described can happen, he thought,
and visualized an ice cube sliding through a cup,
water passing through two slits in a wall:
quantum mechanics in the ensuing pattern of waves.
An hour after they ingested psilocybin mushrooms,
he lifted a cantaloupe in the garden, beheld
its weight, started at the intricate fretwork
on its skin; she touched a peach leaf, recalled
when she wrapped the first peach in white cheesecloth,
the juice on their fingers as they each ate half.
She pinched off tips of budding basil plants
and savored the aroma under her fingernails;
a heron landed near the top of a cottonwood,
but though he half expected a cry none came.
They poured and rubbed oil onto each other's skin;
their sighs and groans made the air tremble,
roil. They erased the plum bruises of a day,
restored themselves at a still point in the waves.

4

Green tomatoes on the windowsill:
if they are exposed to sunlight, will they ripen?

thud: a sparrow flies into kitchen glass;

they planted tulips on the slope behind the kitchen;

"Punks!"

he liked the digging;
she liked the slight weight of a bulb in her hand;

patter of rain on skylight;

they would forget the precise locations
but be surprised in spring;

at the Stop sign,
who slowed and hurled a rock through the window?

as simple as a wavelength;

slivers of glass on the sofa, pillows, rug;

it is impossible to know precisely the velocity and position;

by the time you perceive the brightest yellow of a cottonwood leaf,
it's somewhere else;

yellow hawthorn leaves on the walkway;

shiver, shiver, shiver, shiver, shiver;

who walked from Miletus to Didyma?

he closed and opened his eyelashes along her ear.

5

A point of exhaustion can become a point of renewal:
it might happen as you observe a magpie on a branch,
or when you tug at a knot and discover that a grief
disentangles, dissolves into air. Renewal is not
possible to a calligrapher who simultaneously
draws characters with a brush in each hand;
it occurs when the tip of a brush slips yet swerves
into flame. A woman offers jasmine, dragonwell,
oolong teas: I inhale the fragrances, sip each one,
see chickens in stacked cages, turtles in tanks.
A man hosed blood off speckled white floor tiles
as we zigzagged toward the restaurant; over lunch,
I thought I heard moans and shrieks; when we left,
I glimpsed two white rabbits hauled by their necks
to a chopping block. The glint of the momentary
might dissolve like snow on water, or it might
burst into flame: yellow incense sticks smoking
in a cauldron, a large thin jasper disk that glows
like a harvest moon, the warmth in a glassed garden,
the way our daughter likes to rub foreheads.

6

Cr-rack! She stopped sewing when she heard the rock
shiver the glass window into shards, then the car
revved and sped up County Road 84 into darkness.
The moments you are disoriented are moments
when ink splatters onto the fibers of white paper.
As the area of your ignorance grows, it is possible
the circumference of your knowledge is increased.
Months after a brain aneurysm, when a man whispers
to his wife, "Nothing you do can ever make me happy,"
she turns to the midnight and sobs. When Xerxes
ordered his army to slash the waves of the Hellespont,
he slashed his own fingers to the tendons. Today
we gaze across the Dardanelles—whitecaps on teal water,
a few freighters zigzag down from the Black Sea.
Sunlight flares at the edges of leaves; heat ripples
up from the noon street and from rusted car tops.
The salt in the air stings my eyes: I lift a latch,
step into a patio: bird-of-paradise in bloom;
but, approaching the window, I find peeled paint,
cobwebs; it's dingy inside. I turn, wade into sleep.

7

"Do-as-you're-told scum sucker, you're the reason there are hydrogen bombs,"
yelled at the postal worker
behind the counter—

it leopards the body—

cringes at strangled
anteaters and raccoons hanging in the market—

it leopards the body—

wakes to pulverized starfish in his shoes—

it leopards the body—

disinterred a man and woman
sealed for 1,855 years
under jade plaques stitched with gold thread—

it leopards the body—

winced at hundreds of cicadas stridulating in the umbrella pines—

it leopards the body—

placed a blackbird with a red gash in the trash bin—

it leopards the body—

catches lamb shank in the smoke—

it leopards the body—

recovers a red tulip from inside a corkscrew dream—

it leopards the body—

combusts when they candlelight touch—

it leopards the body—

cars clunk
as they drive off the ferry at Çanakkale.

8

You walk up the steps and find a double peristyle
with a deep entrance porch filled with columns;
at the base of the columns is an octagonal set
of carved dragons, mermaids, and palmettes.
You turn, stride down a dark and narrow vaulted ramp
that emerges with blinding light into a large hall
open to the sky; a continuous frieze on three walls
has a central acanthus flanked by griffins and lyres.
At the far end, roped off by string, is the foundation
of an inner temple with steps that drop to a spring;
when you walk toward this sanctum and look back,
you see stairs to the platform of epiphanies at the rear.
You gaze up to the top of a sixty-five-foot column,
step up to the cord but can't get near enough
to see if the spring is dry or wet. You hunger
for insight into the precarious nature of becoming,
gaze at the woman you love, whet at how passion
is water from a spring, realize that yesterday,
exhausted, you were not going to come this far,
but today, having come, you have sunlight in your hands.

9

Because one stirred the entrails of a goat immolated on an altar,

because a magpie flicks tail feathers,

because blush-red tulips bloomed on the walkway,

because one speaks without fear of reprisal,

because a man—crushed in the debris of aluminum doors, steering wheel,
dashboard, shivered windshield—bleeds and moans,

because he had to visualize black petunias in order to spot Black Trumpets on the
forest floor,

because he slowly bites the back of her neck,

because an eagle glides over the courtyard with outstretched wings,

because a woman fasted, chewed laurel leaves, swayed in noon heat, stammered *the
here is always beginning;*

because she brushes her hair across his eyelids,

because bells tinkle around the necks of goats,

because the ruins of this moment are chalk-white dust in your hands,

because a grain of sand lodged,

because loss is a seed that germinates into *all things are full of gods,*

because a circle opens in all directions,

10

nine purple irises bloom in a triangular glass vase—

a pearl forms in an oyster—

she folds a prayer and ties it to a green cryptomeria branch—

threaded sponges are hanging in the doorway—

a slug crawls along a railroad tie—

a double bass upstairs suffused the house with longing—

silk tree leaflets fold up when touched—

waking out of her coma, she vowed, “I will dip my hands in ink and drag them across white mulberry paper”—

a hummingbird, sipping at a columbine, darted off—

red mullets thrash in the water—

one casts to the end of time—

she wore gold-hooped earrings with her black dress—

urn shards were incorporated into the stone walls of houses—

they swam in the Aegean—

blossoming yellow forsythia is the form and pressure of the hour.

The Ginkgo Light

2009

I

Chrysalis

Corpses push up through thawing permafrost

as I scrape salmon skin off a pan at the sink;
on the porch, motes in slanting yellow light

undulate in air. Is Venus at dusk as luminous
as Venus at dawn? Yesterday I was about to

seal a borax capsule angled up from the bottom

of a decaying exterior jamb when I glimpsed
jagged ice floating in a bay. Naval sonar

slices through whales, even as a portion
of male dorsal fin is served to the captain

of an umiak. Stopped in traffic, he swings from

a chairlift, gazes down at scarlet paintbrush.
Moistening an envelope before sealing it,

I recall the slight noise you made when I
grazed your shoulder. When a frost wiped out

the chalk-blue flowering plant by the door,

I watered until it revived from the roots.
The song of a knife sharpener in an alley

passes through the mind of a microbiologist
before he undergoes anesthesia for surgery.

The first night of autumn has singed

bell peppers by the fence, while budding
chamisa stalks in the courtyard bend to ground.

Observing people conversing at a nearby table,
he visualizes the momentary convergence

and divergence of lines passing through a point.

The wisteria along the porch never blooms;
a praying mantis on the wood floor sips water

from a dog bowl. Laughter from upstairs echoes
downstairs as teenage girls compare bra sizes.

An ex–army officer turned critic frets

over the composition of a search committee,
snickers and disparages rival candidates.

A welder, who turns away for a few seconds
to gaze at the Sangre de Cristos, detects a line

of trucks backed up on an international overpass

where exhaust spews onto houses below.
The day may be called One Toothroad or Six Thunderpain,

but the naming of a day will not transform it,
nor will the mathematics of time halt.

An imprint of ginkgo leaf—fan-shaped, slightly

thickened, slightly wavy on broad edge, two-
lobed, with forking parallel veins but no

midvein—in a slab of coal is momentary beauty,
while ginkgoes along a street dropping gold

leaves are mindless beauty of the quotidian.

Once thought extinct, the ginkgo
was discovered in Himalayan monasteries

and propagated back into the world. Although
I cannot save a grasshopper singed by frost

trying to warm itself on a sunlit walkway,

I ponder shadows of budding pink and orange
bougainvilleas on a wall. As masons level sand,

lay bricks in horizontal then vertical pairs,
we construct a ground to render a space

our own. As light from a partial lunar eclipse

diffuses down skylight walls, we rock and
sluice, rock and sluice, fingertips fanned

to fanned fingertips, debouch into plentitude.
Venus vanishes in a brightening sky:

the diamond ring of a solar eclipse persists.

You did not have to fly to Zimbabwe in June 2001
to experience it. The day recalls Thirteen Death

and One Deer when an end slips into a beginning.
I recall mating butterflies with red dots on wings,

the bow of a long liner thudding on waves,

crescendo of water beginning to boil in a kettle,
echoes of humpback whales. In silence, dancers

concentrate on movements onstage; lilacs bud
by a gate. As bits of consciousness constellate,

I rouse to a three a.m. December rain on the skylight.

A woman sweeps glass shards in a driveway,
oblivious to elm branches reflected on windshields

of passing cars. Juniper crackles in the fireplace;
flukes break the water as a whale dives.

The path of totality is not marked by

a shadow hurtling across the earth's surface
at three thousand kilometers per hour.

Our eyelashes attune to each other.
At the mouth of an arroyo, a lamb skull

and ribcage bleach in the sand; tufts

of fleece caught on barbed wire vanish.
The Shang carved characters in the skulls

of their enemies, but what transpired here?
You do not need to steep turtle shells

in blood to prognosticate clouds. Someone

dumps a refrigerator upstream in the riverbed
while you admire the yellow blossoms of

a golden rain tree. A woman weeds, sniffs
fragrance from a line of onions in her garden;

you scramble an egg, sip oolong tea.

The continuous bifurcates into the segmented
as the broken extends. Someone steals

a newspaper while we doze. A tiger
swallowtail lands on a patio columbine;

a single agaric breaks soil by a hollyhock.

Pushing aside branches of Russian olives
to approach the Pojoaque River, we spot

a splatter of flicker feathers in the dirt.
Here chance and fate enmesh.

Here I hold a black bowl rinsed with tea,

savor the warmth at my fingertips,
aroma of emptiness. We rock back and forth,

back and forth on water. Fins of spinner
dolphins break the waves; a whale spouts

to the north-northwest. What is not impelled?

Yellow hibiscus, zodiac, hairbrush;
barbed wire, smog, snowflake—when I still

my eyes, the moments dilate. Rain darkens
gravel in the courtyard; shriveled apples

on branches are weightless against dawn.

Labrador Tea

Labrador leaves in a jar with a kerchief lid
release an arctic aroma when simmered on a stove.

Yesterday when fire broke out in the bosque,
the air had the stench of cauliflower in a steamer

when water evaporates and the pot scalds.
Although Apache plume, along with clusters of

western peppergrass, makes fragrant the wash,
owls that frequent the hole high up the arroyo's

bank have already come and gone. Yesterday,
though honey locust leaves shimmered

in a gust, no wasp nest had yet formed
under the porch. Repotting a *Spathiphyllum,*

then uncoiling a hose, I suddenly hear surf
through open slats of a door. Sprinklers come on

in the dark; a yellow slug crawls on a rain-
slicked banana leaf; as the mind flits, imbibes,

leaves clothed underneath with rusty hairs
suffuse a boreal light glistening on tidal pools.

Crisscross

Meandering across a field with wild asparagus,
I write with my body the characters for *grass,*
water, transformation, ache to be one with spring.
Biting into watermelon, spitting black seeds
onto a plate, I watch the eyes of an Armenian
accordion player, and before dropping a few
euros into his brown cap, smell sweat and fear.
I stay wary of the red horse, Relámpago, latch
the gate behind me; a thorned Russian olive
branch arcs across the path below my forehead,
and, approaching the Pojoaque River, I recall
the sign, Beware Pickpockets, find backhoe tracks,
water diverted into a ditch. Crisscrossing
the stream, I catch a lightning flash, the white-
capped Truchas peaks, behind, to the east, and in
the interval between lightning and thunder,
as snow accumulates on black branches,
the chasm between what I envision and what I do.

The Gift

The pieces of this jigsaw puzzle
will form King Tut's gold face,

but, at the moment, they are bits
of color strewn on the floor;

these moments of consciousness
have no jigsaw fit—heartbeat

of a swallow in flight, bobcat
prints across the Winsor Trail,

premonition that joy lurks inside
a match, uprooting sunflower stalks,

tipping an urn from a bridge
so that ashes form a cloud.

The pieces of a life stay pieces
at the end; no one restores papyrus

once it has erupted into flame;
but before agapanthus blooms,

before the body scorches, razes
consciousness, you have time

to puzzle, sway, lurch, binge,
skip, doodle, whine, incandesce.

Looking Back on the Muckleshoot Reservation from Galisteo Street, Santa Fe

The bow of a Muckleshoot canoe, blessed
with eagle feather and sprig of yellow cedar,
is launched into a bay. A girl watches
her mother fry venison slabs in a skillet—
drops of blood sizzle, evaporate. Because
a neighbor feeds them, they eat wordlessly;
the silence breaks when she occasionally
gags, reaches into her throat, pulls out hair.
Gone is the father, riled, arguing with his boss,
who drove to the shooting range after work;
gone the accountant who embezzled funds,
displayed a pickup, and proclaimed a winning
flush at the casino. You donate chicken soup
and clothes but never learn if they arrive
at the south end of the city. Your small
acts are sandpiper tracks in wet sand.
Newspapers, plastic containers, beer bottles
fill the bins along this sloping one-way street.

Pig's Heaven Inn

Red chiles in a tilted basket catch sunlight—
we walk past a pile of burning mulberry leaves
into Xidi Village, enter a courtyard, notice
an inkstone, engraved with calligraphy, filled
with water and cassia petals, smell Ming
dynasty redwood panels. As a musician lifts
a small *xun* to his mouth and blows, I see kiwis
hanging from branches above a moon doorway:
a grandmother, once the youngest concubine,
propped in a chair with bandages around
her knees, complains of incessant pain;
someone spits in the street. As a second
musician plucks strings on a zither, pomelos
blacken on branches; a woman peels chestnuts;
two men in a flat-bottomed boat gather
duckweed out of a river. The notes splash,
silvery, onto cobblestone, and my fingers
suddenly ache: during the Cultural Revolution,
my aunt's husband leapt out of a third-story
window; at dawn I mistook the cries of
birds for rain. When the musicians pause,
Yellow Mountain pines sway near Bright
Summit Peak; a pig scuffles behind an enclosure;
someone blows their nose. Traces of the past
are wisps of mulberry smoke rising above
roof tiles; and before we, too, vanish, we hike
to where three trails converge: hundreds
of people are stopped ahead of us, hundreds
come up behind: we form a rivulet of people
funneling down through a chasm in the granite.

Retrieval

A train passes through the Sonoran Desert
when a sudden sandstorm at night sweeps
through the windows: everyone gags
and curses—sand, eddying under the dim
ceiling lights, lodges on eyelashes, clothes,
hair. Memory is encounter: each incident,

a bee thrumming in a hive. You catch
the aroma of incense in a courtyard
but fret you have sleepwalked for hours.
Observing grasshopper legs in a nook,
you brood then exult that a bat roosts
under the eave, yet fail to notice

quince fattening on branches, ache
that your insights may be white smoke
to flame. Though you note toothpicks
at a cash register, an elk head with antlers
mounted to the back of a passing trailer,
you are given a penlight but, within

minutes, misplace it. Without premonition,
striding up a cobblestone street,
through a Pátzcuaro doorway, you spot
a raised coffin with dissolving tapers
by each corner, and harbor a sting
then tang, wax then honey on the tongue.

Tesserae

Picking plums on a ladder, I notice a few
beyond my reach; our neighbor has replaced

the trampoline with cast-iron table and chairs;
black ants on the walkway are encircled

by a horde of smaller ones; we returned
to rose petals strewn on the bed; newly planted

cottonwoods curl at the leaf tips; once I
poked a pin through paper, raised and lowered

the sheet until a partial eclipse came into view;
as a child, I brooded over a *Life* photograph

of bodies piled up in Nanjing; koi mouth
the surface near a waterfall; hours earlier

we lay naked on a redwood deck; black ants
writhe, stiffen; along a south-facing slope,

I find red-capped russulas, aspen boletes,
hedgehogs, a single death cap—deaths form

gaps, no, fissures, in my brain; you crack
a fortune cookie, "Water runs to what is wet."

In the Rose Light

no red-tailed hawk, no crows,
no geese, no raccoon tracks
by the door; when a magpie
flaps across the road,
disappears beyond the window
frame, I ponder frames—
glasses, doorjamb, beehive,
a moment of stillness—trace
an intimate geography:
son in Albany donating a cell
phone so that someone he
will never meet may call
911; clusters of wild irises
in the field; daughter glimpsed
through the doorway, arms
raised, in a ballerina pose,
then, in five minutes, asleep;
though the pink and orange
bougainvilleas are not yet
budding, I incandesce to
our firelight, to the ten years
we have entwined each other.

Qualia

"Oviparous," she says, "a duck-billed platypus
is oviparous." Strapped in her car seat,
she colors an array of tulips on white paper.
Stopped at a light on Highway 285, he stares
at a gas station, convenience store. A man
steps out with a six-pack under his right arm,
while she repeats last night's queries:
Why does the Nile flow north? Who was Nefertiti?

And as cars accelerate, he perceives the silver
one in the rearview mirror will pass him
on the right before he reaches the hilltop.
She sounds out "red": what was the shape
and color of a triceratops egg? Though
a chart can depict how height and weight
unfold along time, no chart can depict
how imagination unfolds, endlessly branching.

As sunlight slants over the Sangre de Cristos,
he notices Tesuque Pueblo police have pulled
a pickup off the highway. At school, lined
up for kindergarten, she waves, and he waves
back. As classmates enter, she waves; and again
he waves back, waves at apple blossoms
unfolding white along a studio wall, at
what is shed and slithering into pellucid air.

The Ginkgo Light

1

A downy woodpecker drills into a utility pole.
While you cut stems, arrange tulips in a vase,
I catch a down bow on the A string, beginning
of "Song of the Wind." We savor black beans
with cilantro and rice, pinot noir; as light slants
through the kitchen window, spring is candlelight
at our fingertips. Ice crunches in river
breakup: someone shovels snow in a driveway,
collapses, and, hospitalized, catches staph
infection; out of airplane wreckage, a woman
identifies the ring on the charred corpse
of her spouse; a travel writer whose wife is in
hospice gazes at a lunar eclipse, the orange moon
at one-millionth of its normal brightness.
A 1300-year-old lotus seed germinates; a ginkgo
issues fan-shaped leaves; each hour teems.

2

A seven-year-old clips magenta lilacs for her mother;

"electrocuted tagging a substation";

patter of rain on skylight;

manta rays feed along a lit underwater cove;

seducing a patient,
he did not anticipate plummeting into an abyss;

over Siberia, a meteor explodes;

"I am happiest here, now!"

lesser goldfinch with nesting fiber in its beak;

love has no near or far.

3

Near Bikini Island, the atom bomb mushroomed
into a fireball that obsidianed the azure sky,

splayed palm leaves, iridescent black, in wind;
that fireball moment always lurks behind

the retired pilot's eyes, even when he jokes,
pours vodka, displays his goggles, medal,

leather jacket hanging from a peg. A woman
hums as she works with willow, X-Acto knife,

magnifying lens to restore a Jicarilla Apache
basket; she has no glimmer a zigzag line

is beginning to unravel, does not know within
a decade she will unload a slug into her mouth.

4

Through a moon gate, budding lotuses in a pond;

"You're it!"

he stressed rational inquiry
then drove south into the woods, put a gun to his head;

vaporized into shadows;

quince and peach trees leafing below the ditch;

succession and simultaneity;

the branch-like shapes in their sheets;

pizzicati:
up the riv-er we will go.

5

August 6, 1945: a temple in Hiroshima 1,130 meters
from the hypocenter disintegrates, while its ginkgo

buds after the blast. When the temple is rebuilt,
they make exit, entrance steps to the left and right

around it. Sometimes one fingers annihilation
before breaking into bliss. A mother with Alzheimer's

knows her son but not where she lives or when
he visits. During the Cultural Revolution,

Xu-mo scrubbed one million dishes on a tanker
and counted them in a trance. A dew point

is when a musher jogs alongside her sled dogs,
sparing them her weight on the ice to the finish.

6

Loaves of bread on a rack; a car splashes
a newspaper vendor on a traffic island.
On the road of days, we spot zodiacal light
above the horizon. Astronauts have strewn
footprints and streptococci on the moon.
Chance sparks the prepared mind: a Cooper's
hawk perched on a cottonwood branch
quickens our synapses. In the orchard,
the sound of apricot blossoms unfolding;
mosquito larvae twitch water at the V-shaped
berm that pools runoff to the pond. We do
not believe we trudge around a flaming
incense burner on a road of years. As fireflies
brighten, we long to shimmer the darkness
with streamers. A pickup veers toward
then away, skewing light across our faces.

7

As light skews across our faces, we are
momentarily blinded, and, directionless,

have every which way to go. Lobelia
flowers in a patio pot; a neighbor

hands us three Bibb lettuces over a fence.
A cricket stridulates outside the window;

and while we listen to our exhale, inhale,
ephemera become more enduring than concrete.

Ginkgoes flare out. A jagged crack
spreads across windshield glass: we find

to recoil from darkness is to feed the darkness,
to suffer in time is—dichotomous venation—

to effloresce the time. One brisk morning,
we snap to layers of overlapping

fanned leaves scattered on the sidewalk,
finger a scar on wrist, scar on abdomen.

II

Spectral Line

1

Who passes through the gates of the four directions?
Robin coughs as she tightens a girth, adjusts saddle,
and, leading Paparazzo past three stalls, becomes
woman-leading-horse-into-daylight. Though the Chu
army conquered, how long does a victory last?
The mind sets sliver to sliver to comprehend, spark;
the mind tessellates to bring into being a new shape.
When the Blackfoot architect unveiled his master plan
with a spirit way leading to a center that opened
to the four directions, I saw the approach to
the Ming tombs, with pairs of seated then standing
lions, camels, elephants, horses lining the way.
I snapped when, through the camera lens,
I spotted blue sneakers—but not the woman—protruding
from the sides of a seated horse, and snapped
a white-haired woman with bound feet munching fry bread.
Peripheral details brighten like mating fireflies.
Then Gloria pointed to the east, gasped,
"Navajos will never set foot here: you've placed
these buildings in the ceremonial form of a rattlesnake."

2

Blinking red light on the machine: he presses
the button, and a voice staggers, "I'm back,"

"I don't know where I am," "I drive but can't
recollect how I get to where I am,"—whiteout

when a narwhal sprays out its blowhole and water
crystallizes in air—"thirty-three days."

He presses replay: the voice spirals, "I lost
four members of my family in a whaling accident";

he writes down numbers, 424-0590, dials,
"My cousin killed himself after his girlfriend

killed herself" ricochets in his ears; though
the name is blurred, he guesses at bowhead

ribs in a backyard, canisters of radioactive
waste stored inland on Saint Lawrence Island;

twenty below: Yupik children play string games;
when he broke the seal on a jar of smoked

king salmon, he recalled his skin and clothes
reeked of smoke from the float-house woodstove.

3

The stillness of heart-shaped leaves breaks
when a grasshopper leaps. I have never
watched so many inch along branches before.
Though they have devastated butterfly bushes,
they have left these lilacs unscathed, but can I
shrug, be marathoner-running-into-spring-light-
over-piñon-dotted-hills? The mind may snag,
still, weigh, sift, incubate, unbalance,
spark, rebalance, mend, release; when one
neighbor cuts grasses infested with grasshoppers,
inadvertently drives them into another's
organic farm loaded with beets, lettuce, basil,
carrots, kale, chard: we cannot act as if
we were asleep; do not entrench boundaries
but work to dissolve them. From light to dark
is a pass of how many miles? Together they sowed
dark millet and reclaimed the reed marsh.
As we entwine in darkness-beginning-to-trace-
light, dew evaporates off tips of grasses.

4

North they headed to Water Bend, what joy awaited them?

"I had to shoot myself or shoot someone else";

cries of snow geese in the wave of sunrise;

the secretary winked, "I'm wearing edible panties";

concubines were immolated on the emperor's death;

the green tips of a leafing apple;

"Here are instructions for when I am dead";

he was retracing the Long Walk;

when we addressed them as *tongzhi,* comrades, they laughed;

she swallowed the white sleeping pills and nearly OD'd;

the spring wind blew the ax off the chopping block;

when confronted with plagiarized lines, he shrugged, "I dreamed them";

the ex-marine checked staff desks at 8:20 for attendance;

from the south, elephants; from the west, horses; from the north, camels;

stepping through the miniature garden, they had no idea
they were writing the character *heart;*

she danced in a topless bar;

when the army recruiting film previewed in the underground bomb shelter,
the crowd jeered;

she surprised him with a jar of Labrador leaves;

"Try to add to the sum total of human culture";

though the edges and angles are many, who knows their number?

5

Acoma Pueblo,
Diné,
Crow,
Oglala Lakota,
Menominee,
Northern Ute,
Zuni Pueblo,
Kiowa,
Muckleshoot,
Standing Rock Lakota,
Muscogee,
Ojibwe,
San Ildefonso Pueblo,
Comanche,
Tlingit,
Mescalero Apache,
Siberian Yupik,
Jemez Pueblo,
Pawnee,
Chugach/Alutiiq,
Mohawk,
Swampy Cree,
Osage,
Taos Pueblo,
Arapaho,
Jicarilla Apache,
Paiute,
Haida,
Onondaga,
Cochiti Pueblo,
Sioux,
Eastern Shawnee,
Caddo,
Santa Clara Pueblo,
Northern Cheyenne,
Prairie Band Potawatomi,
Choctaw,

Chickasaw,
Tsalagi,
Inupiat.

6

We forage for black and yellow morels
under tulip poplars, but they are camouflaged
on the forest floor. Wherever I squint,
I mark varicolored leaves, clusters of deer scat;
at first I zigzag a branch back and forth
under leaves, expecting to uncover some,
then learn to spot-check near the trunks,
forage farther out above the roots among
lichened rocks. We bring two dozen back,
sauté them, add to pasta, salad, sip wine;
but what coalesces in the body for weeks
are glimpses of blossoming redbuds while
driving along a road; horses by the second gate;
lights on the porch; a basket of apples,
bread, farm milk set at a downstairs table;
rocking horse upstairs; two tapers lit;
quicksilver kisses, a diamond light; and,
before, tremor when you felt something odd:
pulled a black tick off from behind your ear,
brushed a smaller one out of your hair.

7

Who rescues hunters tipped into arctic waters?
The hour is a cashmere scarf; as a Black man

near a fountain raises saxophone to his lips
and showers the street with shimmering gold,

red lights of an ambulance weaving in traffic
bob into distance. From a dome, a pendulum

swings, almost touches numbers that mark
the hours in a circle on the floor. When

Robin's coworkers were terminated, she left
her telecommunications job to groom the horses

she loves, even in zero-degree weather; she
cinches a saddle on Nemo even now. A meadow

mushroom, covered overnight under a glass bowl,
releases, onto white paper, a galaxy of

chocolate-brown spores. When you are still,
you spot the chance tracks of the living.

Who can suspend time on a string, make it
arc back and forth while earth rotates around it?

8

Incoming freshmen have been taken hostage,
the letter to the president began; we demand
computers and art supplies; limo service
to the Gathering of Nations; the sum total
of Pell funds be released at once. Benildus Hall
is our headquarters. When the SWAT team
surrounded the building, someone pointed
to the small print: Happy April First.
The mind seizes a spore then releases it.
Descending into the Ming tomb, I discerned
electric lights; a cold iron railing;
people shuffling down steps; camera flashes;
people shuffling across, up the other side,
then out; but nothing was at the center;
only now—the moment when water from six
directions is water from the six directions.
A neighbor listens for wings before dawn;
plums begin to begin to drop from branches.

9

“A driver’s door opened, and a head rolled
out of the burning car”—once she told me,

I could not expunge it. A backhoe beeps
when the driver moves it into reverse, beeps

above the din of morning traffic. A ginkgo
flames into yellow-gold, while, elsewhere,

red tulips flare on a slope. The mind weighs,
balances antinomies: at graduation, a student

speaker carries a black bag to the podium,
unveils bow, arrows, his entire body shaking,

and threatens to take aim at board members—
dissolves into air; a student in the audience

who slurs “far out” after every sentence
dissolves into air; the man who wafts eagle

feather above head, shoulders, along arms,
onto palms—dissolves into air; singers and

drummers who start and end dissolve into air;
and stillness, as we stir to dawn light, breaks.

III

The Double Helix

Marine biologists tracking pods of killer

whales in and out of Prince William Sound
recognize them by their dorsal fins and

by a flood of salmon scales swirling up.
A moose and two calves browse in twilight;

cow parsnip reeks along the road to Fritz Creek.

What does not dissolve in hindsight? The mind
tilts from starboard to port, port to starboard,

but steadies on even keel. Workmen stretch
an orange string to align flagstone steps,

stretch two lime-green strings to delineate

the wall's thickness. Surveying stones
scattered on grass along the ditch, I observe

the wall rise in an irregular wave; and as
we dine at an oval table, discuss how

a diabetic homeopath endures unremitting pain,

how clusters of oyster mushrooms I forage
appear fresh but, when sliced, expose worms,

we lift and turn the incidents until—
a line of dorsal fins breaks water, blows

hang in air—we find their true and living place.

What neither comes nor goes? I try to converse
with a playwright who once sat in Oppenheimer's

chair; propped near a table, nodding before
a color TV—within reach of his right hand,

an oblong box of pills: a.m., noon, p.m., night—

while a slurry of news pours in, he struggles,
fails to string a single sentence, yet, when

I stand, gazes point-blank, extends an arm.
A line of yellow-groove bamboo extends

along a backyard fence. Yesterday we drove

into the Jemez Mountains, cut shaggymanes
along Forest Road 144, foraged among spruce

in mist and wavering rain, and though you
found a site where someone had cut

a bolete stipe and cap, though you spotted,

on a rock, as we drove past, a squirrel gnawing
a chunk of cèpe, we found nothing, but

reveled in the Douglas fir. Look out, look in;
what percolates in the dark? Clouds, rain;

we stretch and align ourselves, become one.

Cries of glaucous-winged gulls on the bay:
in the swirling light at summer solstice,

I mark a plethora in the twenty-five-foot
shift between low- and high-tide lines;

a man casts from shore, reels in small halibut;

red-faced cormorants nest in a cliff side;
an otter lazes with head above waves;

at low tide I wander among squirting clams,
make crunching noises stepping on shells,

flip a rock, find nudibranch eggs,

a gunnel fish; spot orange sea stars,
leather star, sculpin, frilled anemones,

a single moon jelly propelling through
water, worn crab shells at the entrance

to an octopus den, mating helmet crabs

below the tide line; but, before I know it,
the tide swerves back, starts to cover

the far shelf of exposed blue mussels;
gulls lift off; green sea urchins disappear

beneath lapping waves—my glimpse expires.

Skunks pass by a screen door in the dark;
once they ravaged ripening corn in our garden

and still crisscross us because a retired
violinist used to feed them. Once a composer—

a killer whale spyhops near a research vessel—

told a patron, "It's fine if you sleep with
my girlfriend," though he did not yet know

his out-of-town girlfriend had already dumped
him for a software engineer. We pick winesap,

braeburn, golden delicious apples in a neighbor's

orchard, press them; and as cider collects
in plastic jugs while a few yellow jackets sip,

time oozes. In a second I scramble
an egg, blink, scissor string, smudge

a photograph with blue ink, and the trigram

for Water transforms into Fire: when a former
soldier testifies that seeds contaminated

with plague were dumped from airplanes
during the growing season, a knife-edge runs

across my palms, but the truth scalds, anneals.

Fishermen fire at killer whales to prevent
them from stripping long lines of black cod.

You do not need to analyze toxins in peregrine
falcons to ascertain if the web is stretched

and stretched. In a Chimayó orchard where

two horses lean over a gate, two children
offer apples, while someone in a stream casts,

and the line snakes, glistens. Laughter
echoes from a table where someone pours

tequila onto ice, and ice crackles in a cup;

women slice sections of apples and toss them
in a wheelbarrow. We do not heed them

as we turn to each other and effervesce:
are we here to unravel, combust,

lightning the patch of ground where we stand?

Although the passions that torrent through
our bodies will one day vanish like smoke—

these words spiral the helix of living into smoke—
we embrace, rivet, inflame to mortal beauty,

to yellow-gold bursting through cottonwoods,

to morels sprouting through charred ground.
And as sky darkens, absorbs magpie nest,

green water tank, *canales,* pear, quince, slatted
wood fence, we tilt back and forth: though

the time we breathe is millennia when clocked

by a vibrating ray of cesium atoms, seconds
when measured by Comet Hyakutake—the tide

rushes over orange-tipped nudibranchs; silt
plunges underwater into a submarine canyon—

we observe snow on a flagstone path dissolve.

Equator

A bougainvillea thorn catches my sleeve
when I draw the curtain, then something
catches in myself. In Peru, Indians climb
a peak in late June to scan the Pleiades,
forecast the coming season. Meteorologists
have discovered El Niño causes high-level
November winds to blow from west to east,
and the Pleiades, visible low in the north-
east sky only as dawn appears, will dim.
I weigh blue nails, step up to a counter,
buy plastic cement, putty knife, gloves,
wrench, paint thinner—glance at my thumb
already stained black—have no way to
forecast year or hour. Lily pollen smeared
my shirt across the right shoulder when
I moved flowers out of the bedroom
for the night. I try to constellate points
by which I could, in clear weather, hike
across an immense lava flow, but find
elegy and ode our magnetic north and south.

Pinwheel

Firecrackers pop in bursts of white light and smoke;
a cymbal crash reverberates in air: mortality's

the incubator of dreams. Steaming green beans,
or screwing a wrought-iron hook into a post,

I do not expunge the past but ignite the fuse
to a whistling pinwheel. A girl sways under

a lion's head, while others undulate behind
in an *s.* Casting back eight years, we entwine:

a tulip sunlight flares along our shoulders.
At Pergamon, we cross a forecourt—in the center

stands a column bearing an Aesculapian snake,
the space we meander through called the incubator

of dreams. We did not foresee sponges dangling
inside a spice shop or the repeating pattern

of swastikas along walls that have led here.
Though it is Year of the Rooster, I pin *there*

to *here:* a line of dumplings, noodles, rice cakes
disappears; reverberating hail on the roof suddenly stops.

Power Line

As light runs along the length of power lines,
you glimpse, in the garden, watermelon,
honeydew, broccoli, asparagus, silking corn;

you register the tremor of five screech owls
perched on a railing under the wisteria,
shaggymanes pushing up through pecan shells;

though a microbiologist with a brain tumor
can't speak—he once intimated he most
feared to be waiting to die and is now

waiting to die—children play tag in spaces
around racks of bowling balls and white tables,
while someone scores a strike, shrieks;

young girls chassé diagonally across a floor;
a woman lays in an imperfection before
she completes her Teec Nos Pos weaving;

a sous-chef slices ginger, scallions,
anticipates placing a wet towel over dumplings,
as light lifts off the length of a power line.

Grand Bay

Gray Spanish moss hangs from the cypresses—
you stroll on an elevated boardwalk over dry swamp,

step off the platform and take a short path
to a green pitcher plant among grasses: it shows

signs of drought but is larger than your arms
can circle. The streaked pitchers resemble yearning

mouths opening at all angles, in all directions.
An alligator has flattened nearby horsetails,

but, famished, must have headed south.
When you take the boardwalk deeper in, climb

the latticed tower and gaze below, an airplane
lifts from a nearby strip and triggers vultures.

They rise in waves, while a lone hawk remains
unperturbed on a black gum branch. Over a hundred

vultures waver in the sky; while a few soar, most
circle, then resettle on branches. You meander

back out, graze the dangling Spanish moss,
find you choose not to avoid anything that comes.

Departures and Arrivals

An accountant leaning over a laptop
frets: *I have botched this, bungled that*—
he is not focused on numbers or accounts;
a taxi driver at an airport has no time
to contemplate rippling shadows of ginkgo leaves
but swerves between a van and truck;
a reinsurance analyst obsesses over a
one-in-ten probability that a hurricane

will scour the Florida Gulf Coast, while
an air-pollution expert is assigned
the task of designing an early warning
system for a dirty bomb. On an airplane,
waiting out a thunderstorm for two hours,
we cough, sneeze, shuffle, snooze,
flip through magazines, yet find
amethyst in an occasional vein of silence,

think *insulin,* sandpiper tracks on a beach;
and, when we least expect it, a peahen
strays into a yard; over a fence,
a neighbor passes a bag of organic lettuce
left over from farmers' market. As we doodle,
snack, brush spruce needles off caps
of boletes then place them in a grocery bag,
give them to friends, we gaze at a board

of departures and arrivals: Anchorage 2:45,
Boston 1:15, Chicago 11:50, Miami 3:10.
Each moment in time is a hub. In the airport
of dreams, why not munch waffles at midnight,
extemporize, ache, joke, converse with
the dead? *I'm out of it* snaps at the end
of a fiber-optic line, then *sizzles* at
how we thirst and renew our thirst in each other.

Fractal

Stopped at an intersection,
ruminating on how, in
a game of go, to consider all
the possible moves until
the end would take a computer
longer than the expected
lifetime of the universe,
you flit from *piccolo*
to *stovepipe* in a letter,
to scrutinizing faces
while standing in line
at the post office, to weather
forecast—a snowflake
has an infinite number
of possible shapes—
consider, only last weekend,
a wasp threaded along a
screen door in south light,
mark the impulse to—not
see this, do that—water
leafing pear trees along
a curved driveway, relax
the intricate openwork mesh
of spring, recall lifting
a packet of flax seeds
off the counter, and, checking
for an expiration date,
note—red light, green light—
sow when danger of
frost is past, then go, go.

The North Window

Before sky lightens to reveal a coyote fence,
he revels in the unseen: a green eel snaps,

javelinas snort, a cougar sips at a stream.
He will not live as if a seine slowly tightens

around them. Though he will never be a beekeeper,
or lepidopterist, or stand at the North Pole,

he might fire raku ware, whisk them to Atitlán,
set yellow irises at the table, raft them

down the Yukon. He revels at the flavor of
thimbleberries in his mouth, how they rivet

at a kiss. In an instant, raku ware and
the Yukon are at his fingertips. As light

traces sky out the north window, he nods:
silver poplars rise and thin to the very twig.

Yardangs

She who can't sleep takes a sleeping pill,
then another, and another. A crab apple
in the yard blossoms along the curve

of spring. Along a stone wall, we yearn
for a line of Japanese irises that do not appear,
glimpse a body on a stretcher loaded

into an ambulance. In the winter of spring,
a neighbor frets over air-pollution vectors;
a teenage girl worries her horse slashes

its neck along barbed wire. Prevailing winds:
west-northwest. As a physicist posits
all languages have a single root, I weigh

arête, yardang, strike valley, ciénega,
Tsé Bit'a'í: Shiprock, the rock with wings.
But is there bedrock? Scent of your

breasts and hair. Who is of the Bitter Water Clan?
A red tulip in a glass droops within hours.
Tremor at how *z, x, y* puts form into danger.

Virga

A quarterback slants a short pass to a tight end,
and the screen fills with tacklers.
He presses a button—
two miles deep in the Atlantic, shrimp hover around
a vent, where the ocean temperature is thirty-six
degrees—
sips a Lingzhi mushroom brew, dozes:
at a banquet with wineglasses raised, the host starts
to say, "Long live";
teenage girls dressed in red silk
cartwheel past; a line of children trumpet on makeshift
horns;
instrumental in fund-raising the construction
of an elementary school, he has journeyed north
of Yan'an.
Hunting wild ginseng in the hills is rain
that evaporates before it touches the ground;
he has not
seen Orion for a month, nor Sirius, nor read they have
found signs of water on Mars.
Breathing is a struggle:
"I must live along a brightening curve, otherwise
it's fathomless dark";
he considers how his wife and son
will navigate, whether a cousin fencing tomb relics
will reinvent himself;
at an underwater peak
in the Coral Sea, shrimp thought to be extinct
for fifty million years, on a large screen, congregate.

After Completion

1

Mayans charted Venus's motion across the sky,
poured chocolate into jars and interred them
with the dead. A woman dips three bowls into
hare's-fur glaze, places them in a kiln, anticipates
removing them, red-hot, to a shelf to cool.
When samba melodies have dissipated into air,
when lights wrapped around a willow have vanished,
what pattern of shifting lines leads to Duration?
He encloses a section of garden in wire mesh
so that raccoons cannot strip ears in the dark,
picks cucumbers, moves cantaloupes out of furrows—
the yellow corn tassels before the white.
In this warm room, he slides his tongue along
her nipples; she runs her hair across his face;
they dip in the opaque, iron glaze of the day,
fire each emotion so that it becomes itself;
and, as the locus of the visible shrinks,
waves of red-capped boletes rise beneath conifers.

2

A sunfish strikes the fly
as soon as
it hits the water;

the time of your life
is the line extending;

when he blinks,
a hair-like floater
shifts in his left eye;

when is joy
kindling to greater joy?

this nylon filament
is transparent in water
yet blue in air;

grasshoppers
rest in the tall grass.

3

Perched on a bare branch, a great horned owl
moves a wing, brushes an ear in the drizzle;
he can't dispel how it reeks of hunger as he
slams a car door, clicks seat belt, turns
the ignition key. Then he recalls casting
off a stern: he knows a strike, and, reeling in
the green nylon line, the boat turns; and as
a striped bass rises to the surface, he forgets
he is breathing. Once, together, using fifty
irregular yarrow stalks, they generated
a hexagram whose figure was Pushing Upward.
What glimmers as it passes through the sieve
of memory? For a decade they have wandered
in the Barrancas and grazed Apache plume.
He weeds so rows of corn may rise in the garden;
he weeds so that when he kisses her eyelids,
when they caress, and she shivers and sighs,
they rivet in their bodies, circumscribe *here.*

4

A great blue heron
perched
on a cottonwood branch;

tying
a Trilene knot;

a red dragonfly
nibbles the dangling fly
before he casts;

when he blinks,
he recalls their eyelashes;

casting
and losing sight
of the line;

the sky moves
from black to deep blue.

5

Ravens snatch fledgling peregrine falcons
out of a cliff side, but when they try to raid
a great horned owls' nest, the owls swoop,

and ravens erupt into balls of black feathers.
At Chichén Itzá, you do not need to stare
at a rack of skulls before you enter the ball

court to know they scrimmaged for their lives;
when the black rubber ball rebounded off
a hip up through the ring tenoned in the wall,

spectators shrieked, threw off their robes
and fled. The vanquished were tied into balls,
rolled down stone stairs to their deaths.

In one stela, a player lifts a severed head
by the hair, while the decapitated body spurts
six blood snakes. You become a black mirror:

when a woman pulls a barbed cord through
her tongue, when a man mutilates himself
with stingray spines, what vision is earned?

6

Lifting a tea bowl with a hare's-fur glaze,
he admires the russet that emerges along the rim;
though tea bowls have been named Dusk,
Shameless Woman, Thatch Hut—this nameless one
was a gift. He considers the brevity of what
they hold: the pond, an empty bowl, brims,
shimmers with what is to come. Their minds brim
when they traverse the narrow length of field
to their reclaimed pond: they have removed
Russian olives, planted slender cinquefoil,
marsh buttercup, blue iris, marsh aster, water
parsnip, riparian primrose, yellow monkey flower,
big blue lobelia, yerba mansa; and though it
will be three to five years before the full effect,
several clusters of irises pulled out of mud,
placed on an island, are already in bloom.
A bullfrog dives, a bass darts into deep water
as they approach, while, above, a kingfisher circles.

7

They catch glimpses of trout in the depths,
spot two yellow ones flickering at a distance.

He thought a dead teal had drifted to shore,
then discerned it was a decoy. Venus rising

does not signify this world's end. In the yard,
he collects red leaves from a golden rain tree.

Here is the zigzag path to bliss: six trout align
in the water between aquatic grasses, wasps

nuzzle into an apple; cottonwood leaves drift
on the surface; a polar bear leaps off ice.

He does not need to spot their looping footprints
to recognize they missed several chances before

finding countless chanterelles in a clearing.
If joy, joy; if regret, regret; if ecstasy, ecstasy.

When they die, they vanish into their words;
they vanish and pinpoint flowers unfolding;

they pinpoint flowers and erupt into light;
they erupt and quicken the living to the living.

Compass Rose

2014

Black kites with outstretched wings circle overhead—

After a New Moon

Each evening you gaze in the southwest sky
as a crescent extends in argentine light.
When the moon was new, your mind was
desireless, but now both wax to the world.
While your neighbor's field is cleared,
your corner plot is strewn with desiccated
sunflower stalks. You scrutinize the bare
apricot limbs that have never set fruit,
the wisteria that has never blossomed,
and wince, hearing how, at New Year's,
teens bashed in a door and clubbed strangers.
Near a pond, someone kicks a dog out
of a pickup. Each second, a river edged
with ice shifts course. Last summer's
exposed tractor tire is nearly buried
under silt. An owl lifts from a poplar,
while the moon, no, the human mind
moves from brightest bright to darkest dark.

Sticking out of yellow-tongued flames on a ghat, a left foot—

Near a stopped bus, one kid performs acrobatics while another drums—

The Curvature of Earth

Red beans in a flat basket catch sunlight—

we enter a village built in the shape
of an ox, stride up an arched bridge

over white lilies; along houses, water,
coursing in alleyways, connects ponds.

Kiwis hang from branches by a moon

door. We step into a two-story hall
with a light well and sandalwood panels:

in a closet off the mah-jongg room
is a bed for clandestine encounters.

A cassia tree shades a courtyard

corner; phoenix-tail bamboos line
the horse-head walls. The branching

of memory resembles these interconnected
waterways: a chrysanthemum odor

permeates the air, but I can't locate it.

Soldiers fire mortars at enemy bunkers,
while Afghan farmers pause then resume

slicing poppy bulbs and draining resin.
A caretaker checks on his clients' lawns

and swimming pools. The army calls—

he swerves a golf cart into a ditch—
the surf slams against black lava rock,

against black lava rock—and a welt
spreads across his face. Hunting for

a single glow-in-the-dark jigsaw piece,

we find incompletion a spark.
We volley an orange Ping-Pong ball

back and forth: hungers and fears
spiral through us, forming a filament

by which we heat into cesium light.

And, in the flowing current, we slice
back and forth—topspin, sidespin—

the erasure of history on the arcing ball.
Snow on the tips of forsythia dissolves

within hours. A kestrel circles overhead,

while we peer into a canyon and spot
caves but not a macaw petroglyph.

Yesterday, we looked from a mesa tip
across the valley to Chimayó, tin roofs

glinting in sunlight. Today, willows

extend one-inch shoots; mourning cloaks
flit along the roadside; a red-winged

blackbird calls. Though the March world
leafs and branches, I ache at how

mortality fissures the lungs:

and the pangs resemble ice forming,
ice crystals, ice that resembles the wings

of cicadas, ice flowers, drift ice, ice
that forms at the edges of a rock

midstream, thawing hole in ice, young

shore ice, crack in ice caused by the tides.
Scissors snip white chrysanthemum stalks—

auburn through a black tea-bowl rim—
is water to Siberian irises as art

is to life? You have not taken care

of tying your shoes—a few nanoseconds,
a few thousand years—water catlaps

up the Taf Estuary to a boathouse—
herring shimmer and twitch in a rising net—

rubbing blackthorn oil on her breasts—

in a shed, words; below the cliff, waves—
where *å i åa ä e ö* means *island in the river*—

while a veteran rummages through trash,
on Mars a robot arm digs for ice—

when the bow lifts from the D string,

"This is no way to live" echoes in his ears.
Sandhill cranes call from the marsh,

then, low, out of the southwest,
three appear and drop into the water:

their silhouettes sway in the twilight,

the marsh surface argentine and black.
Before darkness absorbs it all, I recall

locks inscribed with lovers' names
on a waist-high chain extending along

a path at the top of Yellow Mountain.

She brushes her hair across his chest;
he runs his tongue along her neck—

reentering the earth's atmosphere,
a satellite ignites. A wavering line

of cars issues north out of the bosque.

The last shapes of cranes dissolve
into vitreous darkness. Setting aside

binoculars, I adjust the side-view
mirror—our breath fogs the windshield.

A complex of vibrating strings:

this hand, that caress, this silk
gauze running across your throat,

your eyelids, this season where
tiny ants swarm large black ones

and pull apart their legs. Hail shreds

the rows of lettuces beyond the fence;
water, running through sprinklers,

swirls. A veteran's wince coincides
with the pang a girl feels when

she masters hooked bows in a minuet.

And the bowing is a curved line,
loop, scrawl, macaw in air. A red-

winged blackbird nests in the dark;
where we pruned branches, starlight

floods in over the earth's curvature.

Begging near a car window, a girl with a missing arm—

Mynah bird sipping water out of a bronze bowl sprinkled with jasmine petals—

Twitching before he plays a sarangi near the temple entrance, a blind man—

Compass Rose

1 Arctic Circle

If the strings of a ¾ violin
are at rest, if the two horsehair
bows repose in their case—
the case holds the blue of lakes
and the whites of snow;
she posts on a horse inside a barn;
rain splatters on the skylight
during the night; she inhales
the smell of newly born chickens
in a stall—if the interval
between lightning and thunder
is a blue dagger, if she hears
Gavotte in D Major as he drives
in silence past Camel Rock—
she stirs then drifts into feathered
waves of sleep; a healer rebuilds
her inner moon and connection
to the earth while she plays
Hangman with her mother;
she stops running out into the cold
whirlpool dark; behind his eyelids,
green curtains of light shimmer
across the polar sky; she has difficulty
posting with one foot in the stirrup—
if he stands, at minus fifteen degrees,
a black dot in the snow—she rides
bareback to regain her balance;
he prays that diverging rays
emanate from a single quartz crystal;
he prays that her laughter be
June grass, that the jagged floating
chunks of ice ease and dissolve;
he prays when she lights a tiny
candle on a shelf; reindeer eat
lichens and browse among marshes

at the height of summer—
if she bows and hears applause
then puts her bow to the string,
if she decides, "This is nothing,"
let the spark ignite horse become
barn become valley become world.

2 Fault Lines

He pours water into a cup: at room temperature,
the cup is white, but, after he microwaves it,

and before steeping a tea bag with mint leaves,
he notices outlines of shards have formed

above the water. As the cup cools, the lines
disappear: now he glimpses fault lines

inside himself and feels a Siberian tiger
pace along the bars of a cell—black, orange,

white; black, orange, white—and feels how
the repeating chord sends waves through him.

His eyes glisten, and he tries to dispel the crests,
but *what have I done, what can I do* throbs

in his arteries and veins. Today he will
handle plutonium at the lab and won't

consider beryllium casings. He situates the past
in the slight aroma of mint rising in the air.

Sometimes he feels like an astronaut suspended
above Earth twisting on an umbilical cord;

sometimes he's in the crosshairs of a scope,
and tiger stripes flow in waves across his body.

3 Glimmer Train

Red-winged blackbirds in the cattail pond—
today I kicked an elk hoof off the path,
read that armadillo eaters can catch
leprosy, but who eats armadillo and eats
it rare? Last night you wrote that, walking
to the stables, you glimpsed horses at twilight
in a field. We walk barefoot up a ridge
and roll down a dune; sip raki, savor
shish kebab and yogurt in an arcade.
Once we pored over divination lines incised
into tortoise shells, and once we stepped
through the keyhole entry into a garden
with pools of glimmering water. In the gaps
between my words, peonies rise through hoops
behind our bedroom—peonies are indeed
rising through hoops behind our bedroom—
you comb your hair at the sink as they unfold.

4 Orchid Hour

Orchid leaves are dark against the brighter glass;
two translucent blooms expand at the tip

of a segmented stalk, and, through the window,
an orange hue limns the Jemez Mountains.

At the lab a technician prepares a response
to a hypothetical anthrax attack, and what

is imagined can be: lionfish proliferate
in the Caribbean, traces of uranium appear

in an aquifer, and the beads of an abacus
register a moment in time: the cost of cabbage,

catfish crammed in a bubbling tank—and words
in the dictionary are spores: *xeriscape, fugu,*

cloister, equanimity. In the orchid hour,
you believe you know where you are, looking

before and through a window, but a pang lodges—
out of all the possible worlds, this, this.

5 The Curtain

Inside each galaxy is a black hole—
        we will never see your birth mother's face—
our solar system has eight, not nine, planets—
        we will never know the place of your birth—
who anticipated five dwarf planets
        in our solar system
        or that ice lodged on one of Jupiter's moons?

When three caretakers brought three babies
        into the room, your mother leapt out of her chair,
        knowing at a glance your face.
We do not want anyone to be like the rings of Saturn,
        glinting in orbit,
        or inhabiting the gaps between rings;
we do not want anyone to be like Uranus.

On a whiteboard, you draw a heart, an infinity sign,
        star, and attune to a gyroscope's tilt.
At night I've pulled the curtain
and stopped at the point
        where you twirled and transfixed—
        but tonight I pull the curtain to the end:
inside our planet is a molten core.

6 2'33"

Land mines in fields are waiting to explode—
from the right lane, a car zips ahead:

you brake, and as it brakes into a left-
turn bay, you glance at the movie marquee

and twenty-four-hour grocery store:
at a checkout counter, a clerk scans

an eight-pack of AA batteries, asks
if you're playing Monopoly; no, no,

and tonight you're lucky: you don't need
a kidney transplant; no one angles a shiv

at your throat—a farmer hesitates
to pace a field before planting yams—

his father's leg tore in a gunpowder burst—
along the riverbed, you spot a few beer

bottles and tire tracks but no elk carcass
in the brush: no snarling dogs leap out—

Orion pulses above the Sangre de Cristos—
and you plunge into highway darkness ahead.

7 Comet Hyakutake

Comet Hyakutake's tail stretches for 360 million miles—

in 1996, we saw Hyakutake through binoculars—

the ion tail contains the time we saw bats emerge out of a cavern at dusk—

in the cavern, we first heard stalactites dripping—

first silence, then reverberating sound—

our touch reverberates and makes a blossoming track—

a comet's nucleus emits X-rays and leaves tracks—

two thousand miles away, you box up books and, in two days, will step through the invisible rays of an airport scanner—

we write on invisible pages in an invisible book with invisible ink—

in nature's book, we read a few pages—

in the sky, we read the ion tracks from the orchard—

the apple orchard where blossoms unfold, where we unfold—

budding, the child who writes, "the puzzle comes to life"—

elated, puzzled, shocked, dismayed, confident, loving: minutes to an hour—

a minute, a pinhole lens through which light passes—

Comet Hyakutake will not pass Earth for another 100,000 years—

no matter, ardor is here—

and to the writer of fragments, each fragment is a whole—

8 Morning Antlers

Red-winged blackbirds in the cattail pond—
today I kicked and flipped a wing
in the sand and saw it was a sheared-
off flicker's. Yesterday's rain has left

snow on Tesuque Peak, and the river
will widen then dwindle. We step
into a house and notice antlers mounted
on the wall behind us; a ten-day-old child

looks, nurses, and sleeps; his mother
smiles but says she cries then cries
as emptiness brims up and over.
And as actions are rooted in feelings,

I see how picking spinach in a field
blossoms the picker, how a thoughtless act
shears a wing. As we walk out
to the car, the daylight is brighter

than we knew. We do not believe
flames shoot out of a cauldron of days
but, looking at the horizon, see
flames leap and crown from tree to tree.

9 Compass Rose

Along the ridge, flames leaped and crowned
from tree to tree. We woke to charred pine
needles in the yard; smoke misted then hazed
the orchard. What closes and is literal,
what opens and is figurative? A healer aligns
her east and west, her north and south.
They backfired fires against the larger blaze—
barrels of plutonium on the mesa in white tents.
We do not circumnavigate but pinhole through it.
She leads a horse past stalls; what closes
and is figurative, what opens and is literal?
Through the skylight she watches a rising moon.
The lines hold, and the fire sweeps south
and north. Sometimes a thistle is just
a thistle. We step out of the sauna and take
a cold plunge; cottonwoods in the riverbed
form a curved flame. Through here,
water cascades; she posts a horse into daylight.

10 Red Breath

Shaggy red clouds in the west—

unlatching a gate, I step into a field:
        no coyote slants across with a chicken in its mouth,

        no wild asparagus rises near the ditch.

In the night sky, Babylonian astronomers
        recorded a supernova
        and witnessed the past catch up to the present,

        but they did not write
                        what they felt at what they saw—

they could not see to this moment.
From August, we could not see to this moment

        but draw water out of a deep well—
        it has the taste of

        creek water in a tin cup,
                        and my teeth ache against the cold.

Juniper smoke rises and twists through the flue—

        my eyes widen
        as I brush your hair, brush your hair—

        I have red breath:
        in the deep night, we are again lit,
                        and I true this time to consequence.

In relief, a naked woman arches and pulls a thorn out of her raised heel—

Men carry white-wrapped corpses on bamboo stretchers down the steps—

She undresses: a scorpion on her right thigh—

A boy displays a monkey on a leash then smacks it with a stick—

Available Light

1

Sandalwood-scented flames engulf a corpse—
farther down the ghat, a man carries fire
in his right hand to a shaved body placed
faceup on logs. He circles five times, ignites
the pyre: the dead man's mouth opens.
Moored offshore, we rock in a creaking skiff,
stiffen at these fires which engulf lifetimes.
A fine soot hangs in the air; in a hotel room,
a woman infected with typhoid writhes,
"Do not let me die," and a doctor's assistant
injects her with antibiotics. Today, no one
comprehends how dark energy and dark
matter enlace this world; no one stares
at the heart-shaped leaves of spring
and infers we are ensnared by our illusions.
After someone cuts the barbed wire across
the arroyo, three-wheelers slash ruts into slopes.

2

Huddled by roadside fires—

“In the end, we’re dust streamers
ionized by ultraviolet radiation”—

teens ditch school and ransack mailboxes—

along the dark street, an elephant lumbers—

cracking a skull with a hammer—

a Yield sign riddled with bullet holes—

metastasized to his brain—

gazing in each other’s eyes,
they flow and overflow—

a one-legged girl at a car window.

3

Along a sculptured sandstone wall, a dancer
raises a right foot to fasten ankle bells;

a naked woman arches and scrubs her back;
a flute player wets his lips and blows.

We try to sleep, but a rat scavenges
on the floor; at dawn, pulling a curtain,

you find a showerhead wrapped in plastic,
crank the faucet: red-brown water gurgles out.

Theriomorphic gods pass through the mind,
but an egret may be an egret. Pausing

at a bomb alert on a glass door, I scan cars
jammed into the square; you hand alms

to a one-eyed woman, whiff red chiles
in burlap sacks. Soldiers cordon off a gate,

set rifles with inverted-V mounts on sandbags.
At dusk, someone on a motorcycle throws

acid at two women and grabs a purse.
A woman wraps a leg around her lover;

dressed only in gold foil, a man gesticulates—
we wipe soot off the backs of our necks.

4

By the acequia headgate, a rib cage—

smoking in a wheelchair,
she exhales and forms a rafflesia flower—

pit bull on a leash—

all men are mortal—

he set his Laundromat ablaze—

the rising spires resembling Himalayan peaks—

"I cannn't talk"—

parrots squawking in the branches of an ashoka tree—

heat death—

when is recollection liberation?

5

Streamers around a bodhi tree, the elongated
leaf tips; under an eave, the hexagonal cells
of a wasp nest. With a wheelbarrow, someone
hauls mixed clay and sand to waiting men.
Once I tilted hawk and trowel, plastered cement
on walls, ran metal lath across the setting coat.
"Their gold teeth and rings burn with their bodies,"
says the boatman. Our love cries vanish into air,
yet my tongue running along your clavicle
releases spring light in the room. Our fingertips
floodgate open: death, no, ardor will be violet
flare to our nights, and the knots of existence
dissolve when we no longer try to grasp them.
The net of the past dissolves when the mixer
stops mixing: cranes stalk fish in shallow ponds;
a woman aligns basil plants in terra-cotta pots;
out of nowhere, a fly strikes a windowpane.

6

At a rink, you step onto ice and mark the lines
already cut, but they are not your lines;
the mind pools what will happen with
what has happened. Moving out and
cutting an arc, you find the locus of creation.
You do not need to draw "nine"
and "four" in ashes to end your attachment
to the dead; you yearn to live as a river
fans out in a delta. A man tosses a pot
of water behind his shoulder and releases
the dark energy of attachment; fires recede
into darkness and become candlelights
bobbing downstream. In this hourglass place,
ants lift grains of sand above brickwork,
creating a series of circular dunes;
two baby robins sleep behind wisteria leaves;
in an attosecond, *here* and *there* dissolve.

7

Lifting off a cottonwood, a red-tailed hawk—
carved in a sandstone wall, a woman applies

henna to her right hand. By the papaya tree,
we climb to a rooftop, peer down at wheat

spread out on another roof—pink and madder
clothes pinned to a line in a backyard.

A bull with a swishing tail lumbers past
the flashlight store; and what is complex

is most simple. In a doorway, a girl leaning
into sunshine writes on the stone floor.

We sip chai in a courtyard, inhale the aroma
of neem leaves laced with diesel exhaust.

I hose new grass by the kitchen, guess
to be liberated from the past is to be

freed from the future; and, as sunlight
inclines, making the bougainvillea leaves

by the window translucent, I catch
our fugitive, living tracks as we make our way.

The Infinity Pool

Someone snips barbed wire and gathers
yerba mansa in the field; the Great Red Spot

on Jupiter whirls counterclockwise;
sea turtles beach on white sand. In the sky,

a rose hue floats over a blue that limns
a deeper blue at the horizon. Unwrapping

chewing gum, a child asks, "Where
is the end to matter?" Over time, a puffer

fish evolved resistance to tetrodotoxin
and synthesized it. I try on T-shirts

from a shelf, but not, twenty months later,
your father's pajamas in the drawer.

Now the stiletto palm-leaves are delineated,
a yellow-billed cardinal sips at a ledge.

By long count, a day's a drop in an infinity
pool. The rose tips of clouds whiten;

someone sprinkles crushed mica into clay
and sand before plastering an interior wall.

Strike-Slip

Faucets drip, and the night plunges to minus
    fifteen degrees. Today you stared at a map
of Africa on a school wall and shook your head
    at "Yugoslavia" written along the Adriatic
coast near the top—how many times
    are lines drawn and redrawn, and to what end?

This ebony bead yours, that amber one
    another's. A coelacanth swims in the depths
off Mozambique and eludes a net; a crystal
    layer forms behind your retinas. Today
you saw the long plastic sheet in the furrow
    blown, like a shroud, around elm branches.

A V-shaped aquatic-grass cutter leans
    against the porch, and you ponder how things
get to where they are. A young writer
    from Milwaukee who yearned to travel calls—
he's hiked the Himalayas and frets
    at what to do: in Nepal, during civil strife,

he and an Israeli backpacker smoked
    and yakked all night in the emptied hotel;
now that the snow is dissolving off Everest,
    bodies of climbers and trash are exposed.
A glowing eel in the darkness—anguish.
    He clacks the beads, *how to live, where to go.*

She wrings her hair after stepping out of a bath—

A portion of a leograph visible amid rubble—

A woman averts her gaze from the procession of war elephants—

Two boys at a car window receive red apples—

Sipping masala tea in an inner courtyard with blue-washed walls—

The Immediacy of Heat

1

No Trespassing is nailed to a cottonwood trunk,
but the sign vanishes within days. You've seen

a pile of sheep bones dumped off the dirt road
to the river; in the arroyo, you've heard gunshots

and veered upstream. On the highway, a pickup
tailgates a new car, and red plastic flowers,

at a curve, fade. In the slanted rising light,
men stumble out of brambles along the bosque

and head into town; and you time your trip
to the drugstore so you aren't accosted

by women hungering for a fix. At the high school,
chains are drawn above the pavement;

the casino parking lot is already dotted with cars.
At the adjoining bowling alley, someone hurls

a strike, and, inside, you lose track of spring.
You catch the clatter of coins—people

blank into themselves. Searching for an exit,
you find you've zigzagged and circled a maze.

2

At the mesa's brink, we eye the road
snaking across the valley toward Pedernal,
where hunters gathered flint. A new moon
and two planets bob in the deepening sky;
I lean into the wind and find this tension
the beginning of a sphere. I bend to a stone
basin and, ladling water, sip. I'm lit
and feel new leaves slide out of branches;
see a child, gathering blue pine needles,
inhale the aroma of earth; a worker
snips and nails metal lath into a firewall.
At our first talk, time grew rounded:
a sparkler scattered sparks in all directions—
though gone, they're gone into my fingertips.
The beauty of imperfection's when a potter
slightly pinches a bowl while arcing it
into a second glaze so that, fired,
the bowl marks a crescent hare's-fur overlay.

3

Under a microscope, I once gazed at algae, at cork cells—

bald eagles at the end of a pier—

a sheep carcass near an arroyo's mouth—

he plants lettuces in the field, and that night it snows—

a woman has closed her eyelids and will never reopen them—

a crow alights on a branch—

the crunching sounds of inlet ice breaking up—

six cars in the driveway—

the invisible lines of isobars, always shifting—

one thing it is to focus; another, to twig—

some of the plastered exterior walls lack the final color coat—

flowering dogwood—

the circular saw rang out through the cambium of summer—

when she vanishes, he will shiver and shiver—

4

Stepping out of the casino, you blink, but lights
still ricochet off glass. *Do not take checks*

from Samantha Cruz is posted on a billboard
by the liquor warehouse. Disorientation's

a rope burn in your hands: are we green flies
drawn to stinkhorns? or shoots leafing

out of time's branches? You blink:
someone hurls a grenade but detonates

himself. You blink: someone in the hallway
at the Bureau of Indian Affairs shouts, "Fire me."

You blink, and a profusion of lavender enters
the window. Dipping under incoming waves,

you resurface with a salt sting on your eyelids.
Once you scavenged a burn for morels.

An unemployed carpenter builds his daughter
a harp; you catch yearning, love, solace

as the forty-six strings are tightened.
You can't pluck them, but the emotions mesh.

5

Vibrating strings
compose matter and force—
as I run a magnetic card

at a subway turnstile, a wave
of people converges and flows
through the gates; people will always

converge and flow
through the gates—always?
If I sprinkle iron filings onto a sheet

of paper, I make visible
the magnetic lines of the moment.
At closing hour,

the manager of a restaurant
sweats and anticipates a dark figure
bursting in and aiming

a gun at his chest, but tonight
no figure appears. In this world,
we stare at a rotating needle

on a compass and locate
by closing our eyes. At dusk
our fingertips are edged with light,

the fifty-four bones of our hands
are edged with light,

and the immediacy of heat
is a spring melt among conifers
gathering into a cascade.

At the Equinox

The tide ebbs and reveals orange and purple sea stars.
I have no special theory of radiance,

but after rain evaporates
off pine needles, the needles glisten.

In the courtyard, we spot the rising shell of a moon,
and, at the equinox, bathe in its gleam.

Using all the tides of starlight,
we find
vicissitude is our charm.

On the mudflats off Homer,
I catch the tremor when waves start to slide back in;

and, from Roanoke, you carry
the leafing jade smoke of willows.

Looping out into the world, we thread
and return. The lapping waves

cover an expanse of mussels clustered on rocks;
and, giving shape to what is unspoken,

forsythia buds and blooms in our arms.

Returning to Northern New Mexico after a Trip to Asia

A tea master examines pellets with tweezers,
points to the varying hues, then pushes
the dish aside. At another shop, a woman
rinses a cylindrical cup with black tea:
we inhale, nod, sip from a second cup—
rabbit tracks in snow become tracks
in my mind. At a banquet, eating something
sausage-like, I'm told, "It's a chicken's ball."
Two horses huddle under leafless poplars.
A neighbor runs water into an oval container,
but, in a day, the roan bangs it with his hoof.
The skunks and raccoons have vanished.
What happened to the End World Hunger project?
Revolutionary slogans sandblasted off
Anhui walls left faint outlines. When
wind swayed the fragrant pine branches
in a Taiwan garden, Sylvie winced, "Kamikaze
pilots drank and whored their last nights here."

Qiviut

A dog's bark has use, and so does honey
and a harpoon. The Inuit use the undercoat

wool of the musk ox, qiviut, to make
scarves and hats. The unexpected utility

of things is a calculus: a wooden spoon,
in a ceramic jar by the stove, has flavors

and stains from tomatoes and garlic,
cilantro and potato broth; it has nicks

and scorch lines, the oil of human hands.
Aspirin may be sifted out of willow bark,

but of what use, other than to the butterfly,
are a butterfly's wings? The weight

of a pin is equivalent to a hundred
postage stamps, and words, articulated

with care, may heal a rift across waters.
An unspoken pang may, like an asymptote,

approach visible speech: it runs closer
and closer but does not touch. As it

runs out of sight, words are mulled:
Venus, a black speck, flies across the sun.

Backlit

You pick the next-to-last apple off a branch;
here's to ripening, to the bur that catches
on your shoelace and makes you pause,

consider, retrace your path. The cottonwoods
have burst into yellow flame; by the ditch,
someone dumps a pile of butchered bones.

When we saw white droppings on the brick porch,
we turned and looked up to five screech owls
roosting on a dark beam, backlit

through wisteria leaves. By the metal gate,
a bobcat bounds off with a rabbit in his mouth.
You yearn to watch sunlight stream

through the backs of Japanese maples
but see sheet lightning in the dark—
it flows from your toes to fingertips to hair.

An aura reader jots down the colors of your seven chakras—

A bus hits a motorcycle from behind and runs over the driver and his passenger—

Discussing the price of a miniature elephant on wheels—

Green papayas on a tree by a gate—

Lit candles bobbing downstream into the sinuous darkness—

A naked woman applies kohl to her right eyelid—

The limp tassels of new ashoka leaves in a tomb courtyard—

Confetti

Strike, rub, crumple—rip paper into shreds:
you can make confetti form a quick orange
blossom before it collapses to the ground.
At night, a driver misses a curve and plows
through the wall into a neighbor's dining room;
twice a day, another neighbor breaks apart
ice with a pick, and her horses dip their heads
into the tub. At dawn, branches scrape,
like rough flint, against the window;
where I stare, a woman once threw a shuttle
back and forth through the alternating sheds
at her loom, and that sound was a needle
sparking through emptiness. Last night,
as sleet hit the skylight, we moved from
trough to crest to radiating wave: even as
shrapnel litters the ground, as a car flips
and scatters bright shards of CDs into the grass.

Spectral Hues

The Chandra telescope tracks
        a particle's X-ray emissions
                before it vanishes into a black hole,

but pin your eyes to earth.
        At sixty, you do not hunger
                to spot an iridescent green

butterfly alighting on moss—
        shift your eyes and it's there.
                A great blue heron lands

on a pond island, and all
        emotions vibrate in spectral
                hues inside the totality

of white light. Driving toward
        the Los Alamos mesas,
                you pass a yellow spot,

where a cottonwood was chainsawed
        after they found
                their son dangling from a limb.

You sprinkle dragon well leaves
        in a glass cup, add simmering
                water, and, after the leaves unfurl, sip.

Windows and Mirrors

Ladybug moving along a cast-iron chair—
translucent pink of a budding lotus
in the pond—you slide along
a botanical wall, recall someone

who stammered to avoid the army
and then could not undo his stutter.
A wasp lays eggs in a tarantula;
a gecko slips under the outdoor grill.

You bite into a deep-fried scorpion
on a skewer: when your father reached
for the inhaler, your mother
stopped breathing. Iridescent green

butterflies pinned to the wall—
a rainbow passing across an island—
striding past ants on a bougainvillea,
you find windows and mirrors

in the refractive index of time.
Tracks of clothes on the floor—
white plumeria on the grass—
hatched wasps consume the tarantula.

Midnight Loon

Burglars enter an apartment and ransack drawers;
finding neither gold nor cash, they flee,

leaving the laundry and bathroom lights on—
they have fled themselves. I catch the dipping

pitch of a motorcycle, iceberg hues in clouds;
the gravel courtyard's a midnight garden,

as in Japan, raked to resemble ocean waves
in moonshine, whirlpool eddies, circular ripples—

and nothing is quite what it appears to be.
When I unlatch the screen door, a snake

slides under the weathered decking; I spot
the jagged hole edged with glass where a burglar

reached through the window, but no one
marks the poplars darker with thunder and rain.

In moonlight I watch the whirlpool hues
of clouds drift over our courtyard, adobe walls,

and gate, and, though there is no loon,
a loon calls out over the yard, over the water.

Point-Blank

Through the irregular mesh of a web,
you shove an inverted vase down
but, instead of trapping a black widow,
squash it when the glass strikes
the floor. Put your fingers
on the mind's strings: in the silence,
you do not grasp silence—a thoughtless
thought permeates you. In Medellín,
a man recalls faces but can't recall
what he wrote or said last night; fretting
at the widening chasm, he runs from X
but does not know if he lunges
this way or to his end. Lifting the vase,
you examine spider legs on the brick floor,
the bulk of the black widow smeared
inside the glass. *A yesterday like today,*
he wrote, and, in his point-blank gaze,
for a second, you are a spider in a web.

The Radius of Touch

Rising over granite cliffs in an aerial tram,
we view the rippling lights of Albuquerque
and volcanoes to the west. At the summit,

the circumference of peaks dissolves
when I blink; and here I am, at a point
where all lines diverge. In the leafless dark,

I can't spot the branches of the golden
rain tree; in the kingdom of touch,
a candle flickers then steadies flame.

Some days are windblown sand stinging
my eyes; others, rice grains in a glass jar.
As matsutake mycelium mantles the roots

of red pine, our cries enmesh each other.
Suspended on cables, we rise up through
the moist darkening air, but the molten

wax of this space dissolves distance.
In the kingdom of scents, the chanterelle
patch we stumbled into flowers again,

and, when I blink, all lines converge.

A cobra rises out of a straw basket before a man plays a bulbous instrument—

Corpses consumed by flames and in all stages of burning—

The elongated tip of a bodhi leaf—

Arranged in a star pattern on a white plate, five dates—

On a balcony, in the darkness, smokers staring at a neem tree—

His head golden, and his sex red—

A naked woman gazing at herself in a small, circular mirror—

At sunrise, a girl rummages through ashes with tongs—

Along the river, men and women scrub clothes on stones—

The Unfolding Center

1

Tea leaves in a black bowl:
        green snail spring waiting to unfurl.
                Nostrils flared, I inhale:

expectancy's a seed—
        we planted two rows
                of sunflowers then drove to Colorado—

no one could alter the arrival
        of the ambulance,
                the bulged artery; I had never

seen one hundred crows
        gathered at the river,
                vultures circling overhead;

I saw no carcass, smelled no rot;
        the angers radiating from him
                like knives in sunlight; I sit

at a river branching off a river:
        three vultures on cottonwood branches
                track my movement;

surrounded by weeds, I cut
        two large sunflower heads off
                six-foot stalks, Apache plume

blossoms near the gate; we wake
        and embrace, embrace and wake,
                my fingers meshed

with your fingers. Nostrils flared,
        I inhale: time, *time*
                courses through the bowl of my hands.

2

A black-chinned hummingbird chick
angles beak and tail out of a nest
woven of spiderwebs and lichens.
Mature, it will range a thousand
miles between coast and highland.
Once you roamed a spice market for chai,
gazed into a mausoleum's keyhole entry
and discovered in synaptic memories
linkages that smoke, linkages that flower.
The owls never returned to the hole
high up the arroyo bank: each spring
clusters of wild irises rise in the field.
Leaning on a cedar bench, we view
fireworks bursting into gold arrays
and tilt on the outgoing tide of breath.
Fireflies brighten the darkening air:
desire's manifest here, here, and here's
the infinite in the intervening emptiness.

3

—Damn, I'm walking on the roof of hell, I need
a smoke, I'm NOT a procrastinator, this sling

nags me, where's ~~my arm won't budge~~ my lighter?
I hobble, fidget, can't drive, I'm a piece of shit

if I can't cast overhead *and unspool that speckled*
fly onto blue flowing water; damn I miss

that bend in the Pecos, I crave Bolivia: when I lift
that serape out of the trunk and *finger*

the cochineal-dyed weft and reach that slit at the neck,
my mind floods, and I need to hang;

I need another drag, at night if my toes
can't *wiggle* out of the sheets and relax,

I can't sleep, and if I can't sleep, I can't ~~fly-fish~~ be—
I'm going to a lodge near Traverse Bay

where a stream *shimmers* with ~~cutthroats~~ rainbow trout;
why, I'm shrinking inside this body,

~~let me out,~~ it's fucking paradise here,
I'll go back in and, after *I needle that willow*

into that Apache basket, ~~under the overhead lights~~
~~I won't have to squint,~~ it will all be repaired—

4

I slice oyster mushrooms off an aspen
then, in the next clearing, stumble
into beer cans and plastic bags.
We cannot elude ourselves; we jump
across state lines where four corners touch,
and nothing happens. A point is a period,
an intersection, spore, center of a circle,
or—"Where are my honeymoon panties?"
a woman mutters, rummaging in her purse—
the beginning of a vector in any direction.

5

The Hubble telescope spots a firefly from ten thousand
miles away. Consciousness is an infinite net

in which each hanging jewel absorbs and reflects
every other. A dog licks her fur, and a green fly

pops out; *homeless*—a teenage girl at a stoplight;
when he ignites yellow cedar in a woodstove,

the float house tilts; they aborted their twins,
and he was forced to bury them by the Mekong River.

Herringbone pattern of bricks on a bathroom floor.
Exhale: spring into sleet here now bursts—

in this world, we walk barefoot on embers, gazing
at irises; she adjusts the light and scrapes plaque

off his teeth; he sips *green snail* tea and discerns
coincident crystals: they tore off each other's clothes—

dipping apple slices into honey, they take a first bite—
inhale: here sleet into spring now bursts.

6

If you light a citronella candle, mosquitoes
can't smell you. A neighbor analyzes air
vectors to prepare a response to a dirty
bomb. Flame on a lake. Diagnosed
with Parkinson's, a man gives notice
to his wife to vacate the husk of their home.
Have I acted without body? You admire
blossoming red yarrow, but a child comes
along and uproots it. After an aneurysm,
a basket restorer leans on a cane at his ex-
wife's funeral; smoke issues from his wrists,
and he barks, "Be wind, flame." Shaggy-
manes push up through grass near a sandbox.
A daughter gives her father a tin flamingo.
During the night, a raccoon lifts the lid
to a compost can, eats. Before first light
strikes the apricots on branches,
you limn human acts in the visible world.

7

Smashing a jewelry case with
a hatchet, he grabs a necklace
from the splintered glass and races

into oblivion. Oblivion is also
digging up carrots in cool
pungent air, cottonwoods branching

along the river into yellow flame;
it's in tropical rain where four
thousand people in an amphitheater,

swaying under umbrellas, chant
poesía, poesía—to the far left
and right two streams cascade the steps:

Vietnamese, English, Hindi,
and Spanish ozone the air.
A warm, waxy light flows across

their skin as they make the rough
silk of love; last night
he gazed at the curve of her eyelids

while she slept. A tiny spider
hangs a web between a fishing
rod and thermostat; a biologist

considers how hydra then algae
then frogs repopulate
a lake covered in volcanic ash;

vultures yank on a buffalo;
somewhere a chigger acts
as a vector of scrub typhus.

8

An architect conceived a rectangular pool
inlaid with stones, and, on three sides,
windows in the building, from ankle
to knee level, pass reflections of sky.
Looking east to the opening, you find
this slit of dreams can't be repeated.
Someone sneezes; a veterinary surgeon,
bicycling to work, is slammed by a car
into a coma. You try shifting the slant
of your pen, the strokes of your ink,
recall when you flung a tea bowl onto
the sidewalk then tried to glue the shards
together. Now hammerhead sharks
whirlpool inside you; in the volcanic
shapes of clouds, visible time; to the driver
who brakes at a red light but rear-ends
his vehicle, the driver shouts, "Horse piss!"

9

—Follow a slate path: you do not come
to an entrance but encounter another blank wall—
I need walls to destroy walls—I ache to give
people ~~azalea~~ persimmon emptiness,
so they can be lit from within: if I place a small

square window in the corner at floor level,
if water spills off a cantilevered roof slab
onto a pool, and you ~~see~~ hear—wait:
what is my grandmother, whisking tea,
saying with her hands: *this is no park*

where bones and teeth are scattered in the grass—
I need to treat my cast-in-place concrete
like ~~sea urchin~~ a folding paper screen—a white
gravel path leads you past another ~~concrete~~ screen—
so it's about walls, light, silencing the noise

of trucks and yells in the street—someone
once stuck a Concealed Firearms Prohibited
sign near my recessed entrance—I detest
bayonets—I need a keyless key—you come
to a ~~circular~~ oval lotus pond, and, in the center—

~~straw mushrooms rise into the visible world—~~
is a stairway that descends to the entrance—
you step into an ~~alcove~~ foyer where, facing
a blank wall, you sit, and, at sunset, *light*
sinks in and grazes your shoulders from behind—

10

The sky lightens behind the heart-shaped
leaves. While we slept, a truck filled
with plutonium lumbered down the highway.
At six a.m. the willow branches swing,
and I tilt on waves. I will tilt when I rake
gravel, uncoil a hose, loosen the spigot.
Green are the lilac and willow leaves;
now my tongue runs along your scar,
our sighs bead, and we wick into flame.
Reflected on glass, a row of track lights
is superimposed on cordate leaves
outside the window. A smallmouth bass
aligns with a cottonwood shadow
in the pond. To wait is to ache, joy,
despair, crave, fret, whirl, bloom, relax
at the unfolding center of emptiness.
I tilt on the outgoing tide of my breath.

11

"Dead? How can that BE?"
A woman sobs as
the airplane taxis to the gate;

flames on water; the whir
of a hummingbird behind my eyelids;
these are means

by which we live: joy, grief, delight—
straw mushrooms
rising into the visible world;

wisps of rabbitbrush are all
that remain of generals' dreams;
a branch of a river rejoins a river;

flip a house and it's shelter,
flip it again and cabinets
open, wine is poured, dogs yap,

people joke and laugh;
sandhill cranes swirl
and descend into a cornfield;

we ampere each other;
a bus stops: a child gets off,
starts walking on a red-clod road:

nothing in sight
in all directions;
a rose flame under our skin,

hummingbird whirring its wings;
a rose flame,
nothing in sight, in all directions:

Sight Lines

2019

Water Calligraphy

1

A green turtle in broth is brought to the table—
I stare at an irregular formation of rocks

above a pond and spot, on the water's
surface, a moon. As I step back and forth,

the moon slides from partial to full
to partial and then into emptiness; but no

moon's in the sky, just slanting sunlight,
leafing willows along Slender West Lake,

parked cars outside an apartment complex
where, against a background of chirping birds

and car horns, two women bicker. Now
it's midnight at noon; I hear an electric saw

and the occasional sound of lumber striking
pavement. At the bottom of a teacup,

leaves form the character *individual*
and, after a sip, the number *eight.*

Snipped into pieces, a green turtle is returned
to the table; while everyone eats,

strands of thrown silk tighten, tighten
in my gut. I blink, and a woodblock carver

peels off pear shavings, stroke by stroke,
and foregrounds characters against empty space.

2

Begging in a subway, a blind teen and his mother stagger through the swaying car—

a woman lights a bundle of incense and bows at a cauldron—

people raise their palms around the Nine-Dragon Juniper—

who knows the mind of a watermelon vendor picking his teeth?—

you glance up through layers of walnut leaves in a courtyard—

biting into marinated lotus stems—

in a drum tower, hours were measured
as water rising then spilling from one kettle into another—

pomegranate trees flowering along a highway—

climbing to the top of a pagoda, you look down at rebuilt city walls—

a peacock cries—

always the clatter of mah-jongg tiles behind a door—

at a tower loom, a man and woman weave brocade silk—

squashing a cigarette above a urinal, a bus driver hurries back—

a musician strikes sticks, faster and faster—

cars honk along a street approaching a traffic circle—

when he lowers his fan, the actor's face has changed from black to white—

a child squats and shits in a palace courtyard—

yellow construction cranes pivot over the tops of high-rise apartments—

a woman throws a shuttle with green silk through the shed—

where are we headed, you wonder, as you pick a lychee and start to peel it—

3

Lightning ignites a fire in the wilderness: in hours,
200 then 2,000 acres are aflame; when a hotshot
crew hikes in to clear lines, a windstorm
kicks up and veers the blaze back, traps them,
and their fire shelters become their body bags.
Piñons in the hills have red and yellow needles—
in a bamboo park, a woman dribbles liquefied sugar
onto a plate, and it cools, on a stick, in the form
of a butterfly; a man in red pants stills
then moves through the Crane position.
A droplet hangs at the tip of a fern—water
spills into another kettle; you visualize
how flames engulfed them at 50 miles per hour.
In the West, wildfires scar each summer—
water beads on beer cans at a lunch counter—
you do not want to see exploding propane tanks;
you try to root in the world, but events sizzle
along razor wire, along a snapping end of a power line.

4

Two fawns graze on leaves in a yard—
as we go up the Pearl Tower, I gaze
through smog at freighters along the river.
A thunderstorm gathers: it rains and hails
on two hikers in the Barrancas; the arroyo
becomes a torrent, and they crouch for an hour.
After a pelting storm, you spark into flame
and draw the wax of the world into light—
ostrich and emu eggs in a basket by the door,
the aroma of cumin and pepper in the air.
In my mouth, a blister forms then disappears.
At a teak table, with family and friends,
we eat Dungeness crab, but, as I break
apart shell and claws, I hear a wounded elk
shot in the bosque. Canoers ask and receive
permission to land; they beach a canoe
with a yellow cedar wreath on the bow
then catch a bus to the fairgrounds powwow.

5

—Sunrise: I fill my rubber bucket with water
and come to this patch of blue-gray sidewalk—
I've made a sponge-tipped brush at the end
of a waist-high plastic stick; and, as I dip it,
I know water is my ink, memory my blood—

the tips of purple bamboo arch over the park—
I see a pitched battle at the entrance to a palace
and rooftops issuing smoke and flames—
today, there's a white statue of a human figure,
buses and cars drive across the blank square—

at that time, I researched carp in captivity
and how they might reproduce and feed
people in communes—I might have made
a breakthrough, but Red Guards knocked at the door—
they beat me, woke me up at all hours

until I didn't know whether it was midnight or noon—
I saw slaughtered pigs piled on wooden racks,
snow in the spring sunshine—the confessions
they handed me I signed—I just wanted it
to end—then herded pigs on a farm—wait—

a masseur is striking someone's back,
his hands clatter like wooden blocks—
now I block the past by writing the present—
as I write the strokes of *moon,* I let the brush
~~swerve~~ rest for a moment before I lift it

and make the one ~~stroke~~ hook—ah, it's all
in that hook—there, I levitate: no mistakes
will last, even regret is lovely—my hand
trembles; but if I find the ~~gaps~~ resting places,
I cut the sinews of an ox, even as the ~~sun~~

moon waxes—the bones drop, my brush is sharp,
    sharper than steel—and though people murmur
at the evaporating characters, I smile, ~~frown~~
    fidget, let go—I draw the white, not the black—

6

Tea leaves in the cup spell *above* then *below*—
outside the kitchen window, a spray

of wisteria blossoms in May sunshine.
What unfolds inside us? We sit at a tabletop

that was once a wheel in Thailand: an iron hoop
runs along the rim. On a fireplace mantel,

a flame flickers at the bottom of a metal cup.
As spokes to a hub, a chef cleans blowfish:

turtles beach on white sand: a monk rakes
gravel into scalloped waves in a garden:

moans issue from an alley where men stir
from last night's binge. If all time converges

as light from stars, all situations reside here.
In red-edged heat, I irrigate the peach trees;

you bake a zucchini frittata; water buffalo
browse in a field; hail has shredded lettuces,

and, as a farmer paces and surveys damage,
a coyote slips across a road, under barbed wire.

7

The letter A was once an inverted cow's head,
but now, as I write, it resembles feet
planted on the earth rising to a point.

Once is glimpsing the Perseid meteor shower—
and, as emotion curves space, I find
a constellation that arcs beyond the visible.

A neighbor brings cucumbers and basil;
when you open the bag and inhale, the world
inside is fire in a night courtyard

at summer solstice; we have limned the time here
and will miss the bamboo arcing along
the fence behind our bedroom, peonies

leaning to earth. A *mayordomo* retrenches
the opening to the ditch; water runs near
the top of juniper poles that line our length—

in the bosque, the elk carcass decomposes
into a stench of antlers and bones. Soon
ducks will nest on the pond island, and as

a retired violinist who fed skunks left a legacy—
one she least expected—we fold this
in our pocket and carry it wherever we go.

Stilling to North

Just as the blue tip of a compass needle
stills to north, you stare at a pencil

with sharpened point, a small soapstone
bear with a tiny chunk of turquoise

tied to its back, the random pattern
of straw flecked in an adobe wall;

you peruse the silver poplar branches,
the spaces between branches, and as

a cursor blinks, situate at the edge
of loss—the axolotl was last sighted

in Xochimilco over twenty years ago;
a jaguar meanders through tawny

brush in the Gila Wilderness—
and, as the cursor blinks, you guess

it's a bit of line that arcs—a parsec
made visible—and as you sit,

the imperfections that mark you
attune you to a small emptied flask

tossed to the roadside and the X,
never brewed, that throbs in your veins.

—No one could anticipate this distance from Monticello—

Westbourne Street

Porch light illuminating white steps, light
over a garage door, darkness inside windows—
and the darkness exposes the tenuous.
A glassblower shapes a rearing horse
that shifts, on a stand, from glowing orange
to glistening crystal; suddenly the horse

shatters into legs, head, body, mane.
At midnight, "Fucking idiot!" a woman yells,
shaking the house; along a hedge,
a man sleeps, coat over head, legs sticking out;
and, at eight a.m., morning glories open
on a fence; a backhoe heads up the street.

From this window, he views banana leaves,
an orange tree with five oranges, houses
with shingled roofs, and steps leading
to an upstairs apartment; farther off, palm trees,
and, beyond, a sloping street, ocean, sky;
but what line of sight leads to revelation?

Cloud Hands

A woman moves through a Cloud Hands position,
    holding and rotating

an invisible globe—thud, shattering glass, moan,
    horn blast—so many

worlds to this world—two men dipnet
    sockeye salmon

at the mouth of a river—from a rooftop, a seagull
    squawks and cries;

a woman moves through Grasp the Bird's Tail—
    someone on a stretcher

is wheeled past glass doors—a desert fivespot
    rises in a wash—

and, pressing her tongue to the roof
    of her mouth,

she focuses, in the near distance, on the music
    of sycamore leaves.

In the Bronx

Crossing a street, you hear the cry of a strawberry finch,
                    and, reaching the curb,

catch the smell of a young pig that, minutes ago,
                    hurtled across the trail;

inhaling a chocolate scent, you approach a small orchid;
                    nearby, two streaked

pitcher plants have opened lids but opened laterally;
                    a fern rises out

of the crotch of an ʻōhiʻa tree, and droplets have collected
                    on a mule's foot fern;

up on the ridge, sliding mist veils the palms and eucalyptus;
                    nearby, a trumpet tree

dangles orange-scented blooms; you stare at the crack
                    in a blue marble tree,

at a maze of buttressed roots, just as a man holding
                    a placard, waving people

toward a new doughnut shop, turns and, thud, a wild avocado
                    has dropped to the ground.

Unpacking a Globe

I gaze at the Pacific and don't expect
to ever see the heads on Easter Island,

though I guess at sunlight rippling
the yellow grasses sloping to shore;

yesterday a doe ate grass in the orchard:
it lifted its ears and stopped eating

when it sensed us watching from
a glass hallway—in his sleep, a veteran

sweats, defusing a land mine.
On the globe, I mark the Battle of

the Coral Sea—no one frets at that now.
A poem can never be too dark,

I nod and, staring at the Kenai, hear
ice breaking up along an inlet;

yesterday a coyote trotted across
my headlights and turned his head

but didn't break stride; that's how
I want to live on this planet:

alive to a rabbit at a glass door—
and flower where there is no flower.

—During the Cultural Revolution, a boy saw his mother shot by a firing squad—

Traversal

At dawn you dip oars in water, row out
    on a lake—the oarlocks creak—and, drifting,

inhale the pines along the shore. A woman
    puts water in a pot, lights a stove: before

it steams, she looks out at the glimmering:
    between two points, we traverse an infinite set

of paths: here we round a bend in an arroyo
    and stumble onto two sheep carcasses;

here peonies and ranunculus unfold in a vase.
    The day has the tensile strength of silk:

you card the hours, spin them, dip
    the skeins in a dye pot, and grief or anger,

pleasure or elation's the mordant that fixes
    the hue. You find yourself stepping

through a T-shaped doorway: the niches
    in a circular ruin mark the sun's motion;

a woman fries potatoes in a pan and finds,
    in the night, mice have slipped through

a hole under the sink and nibbled soap
    in a dish; a returning hunter pulls a screen

latch but, hearing a rattlesnake inside,
    slams it, stares through the vibrating mesh.

The Radiant's

the origin point of a meteor shower.
        Peaches redden: branches
                are propped with juniper posts

and a shovel; steam rises
        from a caldera; stepping
                through a lava tube, we emerge

into a rain forest dotted
        with wild ginger; desire
                branches like mycelium.

Carrying a bolete in a basket,
        we forage under spruce and fir
                in cool alpine air;

a plume rises where lava reaches
        the ocean. Who said, *Out of nothing,*
                nothing can come? We do not lie

in a meadow to view the Perseids
        but discover, behind a motel,
                a vineyard, and gather as we go.

Doppler Effect

Stopped in cars, we are waiting to accelerate
along different trajectories. I catch the rising

pitch of a train—today one hundred nine people
died in a stampede converging at a bridge;

radioactive water trickles underground
toward the Pacific Ocean; nickel and copper

particulates contaminate the Brocade River.
Will this planet sustain ten billion people?

Ah, switch it: a spider plant leans toward
a glass door, and six offshoots dangle from it;

the more I fingered the clay slab into a bowl,
the more misshapen it became; though I have

botched *this,* bungled *that,* the errancies
reveal it would not be better if things happened

just as I wished; a puffer fish inflates on deck;
a burst of burnt rubber rises from pavement.

Adamant

Deer browse at sunrise in an apple orchard,
while honey locust leaves litter the walk.
A neighbor hears gunshots in the bosque

and wonders who's firing at close range;
I spot bear prints near the Pojoaque River
but see no sign of the reported mountain lion.

As chlorophyll slips into the roots of a cottonwood
and the leaves burst into yellow-gold, I wonder,
where's our mortal flare? You can travel

to where the Tigris and Euphrates flow together
and admire the inventions of people living
on floating islands of reeds; you can travel

along an archipelago and hike among volcanic
pools steaming with water and sulfuric acid;
but you can't change the eventual, adamant body.

Though death might not come like a curare-
dipped dart blown out of a tube or slam
at you like surf breaking over black lava rock,

it will come—it *will* come—and it unites us—
brother, sister, boxer, spinner—in this pact,
while you inscribe a letter with trembling hand.

—A woman detonates when a spam text triggers bombs strapped to her body—

Python Skin

1

Smoke engulfs a boat in the harbor—we motor
past and recall a flotilla of fishing boats

lashed together and Hong Kong skyscrapers
in the distance—when we dock, I continue

to bob and smell diesel fumes on water;
though medical researchers extract saliva

from Gila monsters, draw blue blood
from horseshoe crabs, seeding a cloud

is never a cure; on a fireplace mantel,
a flame sways then steadies above a pool

of wax, and a tuberose aroma fills the room;
at sunrise, I spot a grapevine leafing out:

though no coyote slants across the field
with a rabbit in its mouth, though no grenade

is hurled over here, I recall fires crackling
in jagged lines along a ridge to the west,

apple trees out the window vanishing in smoke—
haze wherever we look, think, run, stop, be.

2

Beer bottles and diapers thrown out of car windows—
    you carry a shovel down to the cattail pond where,
each spring, someone cuts a channel and drains
    water into the nearby acequia; you patch the channel
but know by summer it will be cut open again;

no one ever knows who does this; you never meet
    the lab technician who works on bombs—*I work*
on sound: sound waves are odd when they
    turn a corner, and their wavelengths stretch,
and you compartmentalize and list your errands:

post office, meeting with water lawyer, buy apples
    and yogurt for lunch; and barely notice a hummingbird
darting from columbine to columbine; an accountant
    yearns to stroll in a meadow, inhale the alpine
air, listen to water cascading between rocks,

but he squints at numbers in columns; and a lawyer
    dates his boss but one day he handcuffs and assaults her,
breaks two bones in her face as she begs for her life—
    in jail he takes the prison razor given him to shave,
disassembles it, then slits his throat in the night.

3

The housewives of Königsberg set their kitchen
clocks to when a philosopher walked by the window;

a daily timed walk is a single violin string
out of which all waves rise and fall—deep-fried

crabs are immersed in a basket of Sichuan chiles;
at a subway juncture, a man bows an erhu,

and a melody reverberates down the walkways;
the outlines of branches emerge out of the dark—

I peruse the pale eyes of a cuttlefish crammed
into a tank: what if you ask the vibrating

python skin of an erhu how it feels to make sound—
what if salt or a lichen or the erhu spoke?

4

A cat drops a downy woodpecker at the door—
        one day a man wakes to a pain in his chest
and requires a quadruple bypass—he eats
        fry bread for lunch; you scan a black
locust whose last branch failed to leaf this spring;

though acknowledging grief assuages the pain,
        red dye droplets splash into water and swirl
before vanishing from sight; though the locust
        will be stacked as firewood, you observe mounds
ants make in the courtyard and recognize how

their channels of empty spaces extend vital breath;
        you do not sense impending doom but deep-
water the cottonwood that survived a drought
        and shades the house; in an erhu melody
filling the subway walkway, you catch the tremor

of python skin but apprehend another python
        snag on a branch and peel off a layer;
as the two strings evoke shadows of candles
        flickering red, you gather wild irises
out of the air and peel off *mine, yours, his, hers:*

5

flitting to the honeysuckle, a white butterfly—

when she scribbles a few phrases by candlelight, a peony buds—

two does bound up from the apple orchard—

he sprays a paper-wasp nest under the portal—

sunlight touches the highest leaves of the silver poplars—

a buck scrapes his rack on a slender aspen trunk—

you slow but drive steadily through a hailstorm until it clears—

walkingstick on the screen door—

swimming back to shore, they spot a few turtles in the shallows—

we stroll up an arroyo then glance back at the S-curve of trees in the valley—

the steady hum of cars driving men to the lab—

red-winged blackbirds nesting in the cattails—

here a peony buds and fragrances the air—

he kisses the back of her neck, and she nestles along his body—

in the sky, not a shred of cloud—

Lichen Song

—Snow in the air   you've seen a crust on the ceiling wood and never considered how I gather moisture when you step out of the shower   you don't care that I respire as you breathe   for years you've washed your face gazed in the mirror shaved combed your hair rushed out while I who may grow an inch in a thousand years catch the tingling sunlight   you don't understand how I can dive to a temperature of liquefied gas and warm back up absorb water start growing again without a scar   I can float numb in space be hit with cosmic rays then return to Earth and warm out of my sleep to respire again without a hiccup   you come and go while I stay gripped to pine and the sugar of existence runs through you runs through me you sliver if you just go go go   if you slowed you could discover that mosquitoes bat their wings six hundred times a second and before they mate synchronize their wings you could feel how they flicker with desire   I am flinging your words and if you absorb not blot my song you could learn you are not alone in pain and grief though you've instilled pain and grief   you can urge the dare and thrill of bliss if and when you stop to look at a rock at a fence post but you cough only look yes look at me now because you are blink about to leave—

Black Center

Green tips of tulips are rising out of the earth—
you don't flense a whale or fire at beer cans

in an arroyo but catch the budding
tips of pear branches and wonder what

it's like to live along a purling edge of spring.
Jefferson once tried to assemble a mastodon

skeleton on the White House floor but,
with pieces missing, failed to sequence the bones;

when the last speaker of a language dies,
a hue vanishes from the spectrum of visible light.

Last night, you sped past revolving and flashing
red, blue, and white lights along the road—

a wildfire in the dark; though no one
you knew was taken in the midnight ambulance,

an arrow struck a bull's-eye and quivered
in its shaft: one minute gratitude rises

like water from an underground lake;
another, dissolution gnaws from a black center.

Under a Rising Moon

Driving at night between Chinle and Tsaile,
I fixate on deer along the road: in the headlights,
they're momentarily blinded but could leap out.
An unglazed pot fired and streaked from ash
will always bear the beauty of chance, while
a man who flies by helicopter and lands
on an iceberg will always bear the crunching
sounds under his feet. This morning we hiked
from the rim down to White House Ruins,
and the scraping of cottonwood leaves
is still in my ears. *Diné women tied their infants*
on cradleboards, stashed them in crevices
but never came back. Though warned of elk,
I heed the car with a single headlight enlarging
in my rearview mirror—when the mind
is sparked with pixels, it's hard to swerve
and brake. The Anasazi must have marveled
at the whitening sheen on the cliff, but tonight
tracks of moonlight run ahead of where I can be.

Light Echoes

In the parking lot, we look up at the Milky Way:
a poacher aims a rifle at a black rhinoceros:

a marble boat disappears in smog.
As I gaze at an anthurium, wild cockatoos

cry from the tops of blue marble trees;
a lake forms on an ice sheet: rivers branch

and branch. A guitarist leans into the space
between notes; a stone plummets

down a black well: he does not know
the silence when he will aim a bullet

at himself. On a wall, a red spider;
macaws in cages squawk when we approach:

I scratch letters into the leaf of an autograph tree.
Like lights extending along a bay,

notes from Norteña splay in my ears—
they sparkle then disappear into black sounds.

First Snow

A rabbit has stopped on the gravel driveway:

imbibing the silence,
you stare at spruce needles:

there's no sound of a leaf blower,
no sign of a black bear;

a few weeks ago, a buck scraped his rack
against an aspen trunk;
a carpenter scribed a plank along a curved stone wall.

You only spot the rabbit's ears and tail:

when it moves, you locate it against speckled gravel,
but when it stops, it blends in again;

the world of being is like this gravel:

you think you own a car, a house,
this blue-zigzagged shirt, but you just borrow these things.

Yesterday, you constructed an aqueduct of dreams
and stood at Gibraltar,
but you possess nothing.

Snow melts into a pool of clear water;
and, in this stillness,

starlight behind daylight wherever you gaze.

—Salt cedar rises through silt in an irrigation ditch—

Courtyard Fire

At autumn equinox,
we make a fire
in the courtyard: sparks

gust into the black air,
and all seasons are enfolded
in these flames:

snow gathers and tips the lilac twigs;
a stinkhorn rises
out of dirt below a waterspout;

ants climb the peony stalks;
and, gazing into coals,
I skydive and pass through

stages of youth: at first,
I climb a tower and,
looking out, find the world tipped;

then I dash through halls:
if ripening is all,
what can the dead teach us?

We who must rage and lust,
hurtle zigzagging between cars
in traffic, affirm

the call to abandon illusions
is a call to abandon
a condition that requires illusions;

and, as I pull the cord,
spring rips and blooms;
on landing, I sway on earth.

White Sands

—Walking along a ridge of white sand—
it's cooler below the surface—

we stop and, gazing at an expanse
of dunes to the west,
watch a yellow yolk of sun drop to the mountains—

an hour earlier, we rolled down a dune,
white sand flecked your eyelids and hair—

a claret cup cactus blooms,
and soaptree yuccas
move as a dune moves—

so many years later, on a coast, waves rolling to shore,
wave after wave,

I see how our lives have unfolded,
a sheen of
wave after whitening wave—

and we are stepping barefoot,
rolling down a dune, white flecks on our lips,

on our eyelids: we are lying in a warm dune
as a full moon
lifts against an ocean of sky—

Salt Song

Zunis make shrines on the way to a lake where I emerge   and Miwoks gather me out of pools along the Pacific   the cheetah thirsts for me   and when you sprinkle me on rib eye you have no idea how I balance silence with thunder in crystal   you dream of butterfly hunting in Madagascar   spelunking through caves echoing with dripping stalactites   and you don't see how I yearn to shimmer an orange aurora against flame   look at me in your hand   in Egypt I scrubbed the bodies of kings and queens   in Pakistan I zigzag upward through twenty-six miles of tunnels before drawing my first breath in sunlight   if you heat a kiln to 2380 degrees and scatter me inside   I vaporize and bond with clay   in this unseen moment a potter prays because my pattern is out of his hands   and when I touch your lips   you salivate   and when I dissolve on your tongue   your hair rises   ozone unlocks   a single stroke of lightning sizzles to earth.

—The plutonium waste has been hauled to an underground site—

Sprang

1 Winter Stars

You will never forget corpses wrapped in flames—
at dusk, you watched a congregation of crows

gather in the orchard and sway on branches;
in the dawn light, a rabbit moves and stops,

moves and stops along the grass; and as
you pull a newspaper out of a box, glance

at the headlines, you feel the dew on grass
as the gleam of fading stars: yesterday you met

a body shop owner whose father was arrested,
imprisoned, and tortured in Chile, heard

how men were scalded to death in boiling water;
and, as the angle of sunlight shifts, you feel

a seasonal tilt into winter with its expanse
of stars—candles flickering down the Ganges,

where you light a candle on a leaf and set it
flickering, downstream, into darkness—

dozens of tiny flames flickering into darkness—
then you gaze at fires erupting along the shore.

2 Hole

No sharp-shinned hawk perches
on the roof rack of his car and scans
for songbirds; the reddening ivy
along a stone wall deepens in hue;
when he picks a sungold tomato
in the garden and savors
the burst in his mouth, he catches
a mock orange spray in the air;
and as he relights the pilot
to a water heater, checks thermostats,
the sound of water at a fountain
is prayer; earlier in the summer,
he watched a hummingbird land,
sip water, and douse its wings,
but, now, a widening hole gnaws
at that time; and, glancing
at a spotted towhee nest on a lintel,
he knows how hunting chanterelles
at the ski basin and savoring
them at dinner is light-years away.

3 Talisman

Quetzal: you write
the word on a sheet of paper
then erase it;

each word, a talisman,
leaves a track: a magpie
struts across a portal

and vanishes from sight;
when you bite into sea urchin,
ocean currents burst

in your mouth; and when
you turn, view the white shutters
to the house,

up the canyon, a rainbow
arcs into clouds;
expectancies, fears, yearnings—

hardly bits of colored glass
revolving in a kaleidoscope—
mist rising from a hot spring

along a river: suddenly
you are walking toward Trinity Site
searching for glass

and counting minutes
of exposure under the sun;
suddenly small things ignite.

4 *Kintsugi*

He slips on ice near a mailbox—

no gemsbok leaps across the road—

a singer tapped an eagle feather on his shoulders—

women washed indigo-dyed yarn in this river, but today gallium and germanium
particles are washed downstream—

once they dynamited dikes to slow advancing troops—

picking psilocybin mushrooms and hearing cowbells in the mist—

as a child, he was tied to a sheep and escaped marauding soldiers—

an apple blossom opens to five petals—

as he hikes up a switchback, he remembers undressing her—

from the train window, he saw they were on ladders cutting fruit off cacti—

in the desert, a crater of radioactive glass—

assembling shards, he starts to repair a gray bowl with gold lacquer—

they ate psilocybin mushrooms, gazed at the pond, undressed—

hunting a turkey in the brush, he stops—

from the ponderosa pines: *whoo-ah, whoo whoo whoo—*

5 Yellow Lightning

In the five a.m. dark, a car with bright lights
and hazard lights blinking drives directly at me;
veering across the yellow lines, I pass by it

and exhale: amethyst crystals accrete
on a string: I will live to see pear
blossoms in the orchard, red-winged black-

birds nesting in the cattails; I love the sighs
you make when you let go—my teeth gripping
your earlobe—pearls of air rising through water—

and as a white moon rising over a canyon
casts pine shadows to the ground, gratitude
rivers through me: sharpened to starlight,

I make our bed and find your crystal
between the sheets; and when I part the curtains,
daylight's a strobe of yellow lightning.

6 Red-Ruffed Lemur

You locate a spotted-towhee nest on a beam,
peony shoots rising out of the earth, but a pang
surges in your blood with each systole—
though spring emerges, the forsythia eludes you—
in a coffee shop, a homeless man gathers
a Chinese magazine and two laundered towels
in a clear plastic bag, mutters "Metro,"
and heads out the door—a bird trills
in the blue spruce, but when it stops, the silence
is water running out of thawing glacial ice;
and you mix cement in a wheelbarrow,
haul it, in a bucket, up a ladder to a man
on a rooftop plastering a parapet—cherry buds
unfurl along a tidal basin—a red-ruffed
lemur squints out of a cage at human faces,
shudders, and scurries back into a hole—
and you surge at what's enfolded in this world:

7 *This Is the Writing, the Speaking of the Dream*

red bougainvillea blooming against the glass—

she likes it when he pulls her to him—

once you saw murres crowding the cliffs of an arctic island—

thousands of blue-black mussels, exposed and gripping rocks at low tide—

he runs his fingers between her toes—

light reflecting off snow dazzles their eyes—

a tiger shark prowls along the shoreline for turtles—

an aspen leaf drops into a creek—

when he tugs the roots of her hair, he begins to tiger—

this is the writing, the speaking of the dream—

no one knows why ten thousands of murres are dying—

he hungers for sunlight to slant along their bodies on a Molokaʻi slope—

sunlight streams as gold-flecked koi roil the waters and churn—

they roil the waters and churn—

killer whales move through Prince William Sound—

8 Net Light

Poised on a bridge, streetlights
on either shore, a man puts
a saxophone to his lips, coins
in an upturned cap, and a carousel

in a piazza begins to turn:
where are the gates to paradise?
A woman leans over an outstretched
paper cup—leather workers sew

under lamps: a belt, wallet, purse—
leather dyed maroon, beige, black—
workers from Seoul, Lagos, Singapore—
a fresco on a church wall depicts

the death of a saint: a friar raises
both hands in the air—on an airplane,
a clot forms in a woman's leg
and starts to travel toward her heart—

a string of notes riffles the water;
and, as the clot lodges, at a market
near lapping waves, men unload
sardines in a burst of argentine light.

9 Sprang

Before tracking pods of killer whales
in Prince William Sound, she reads a poem

on deck to start each day. In solstice light,
a moose lumbers across a driveway; I mark

orange and purple sea stars exposed at low tide,
the entrance to an octopus den. Astronomers

have observed two black holes colliding;
and, though the waves support relativity,

we need no equation to feel the sprang of space
and time. A marine biologist gives everything

away, weaves her coffin out of alder branches,
lines it with leaves; a carpenter saws kiln-

dried planks to refurbish a porch; I peruse
the tips of honeycrisp apples we planted

last fall, and, though no blossoming appears,
the air is rife with it; the underground

stirs, and I can only describe it by saying
invisible deer move through an orchard in bloom.

—A man who built plutonium triggers breeds horses now—

Transfigurations

Though neither you nor I saw flowering pistachio trees
in the Hanging Gardens of Babylon, though neither
you nor I saw the Tigris River stained with ink,
though we never heard a pistachio shell dehisce,
we have taken turns holding a panda as it munched
on bamboo leaves, and I know that rustle now.
I have awakened beside you and inhaled August
sunlight in your hair. I've listened to the scroll
and unscroll of your breath—dolphins arc along
the surface between white-capped waves; here,
years after we sifted yarrow and read from the *Book*
of Changes, I mark the dissolving hues in the west
as the sky brightens above overhanging willows.
The panda fidgets as it pushes a stalk farther
into its mouth. We step into a clearing with budding
chanterelles; and, though this space shrinks and
is obscured in the traffic of a day, *here* is the anchor
I drop into the depths of teal water. I gaze deeply
at the panda's black patches around its eyes;
how did it evolve from carnivore to eater of bamboo?
So many transfigurations I will never fathom.
The arc of our lives is a brightening then dimming,
brightening then dimming—a woman catches
fireflies in an orchard with the swish of a net.
I pick an openmouthed pistachio from a bowl
and crack it apart: a hint of Assyria spills
into the alluvial fan of sunlight. I read spring in
autumn in the scroll of your breath; though
neither you nor I saw the completion of the Great Wall,
I wake to the unrepeatable contour of this breath.

Dawn Redwood

Early morning light: a young red-tailed hawk
    glided onto an overhead branch and peered

down at me, but it did not look with your eyes—
    a battered and rusted pickup lies in the wash;

Navajo tea buds on the trail—I headed back
    and checked, in the boiler room, the traps,

baited with peanut butter—now a gnat
    flits against this lit screen: where are you now?

One morning, we walked in a Rhode Island
    cemetery and did not look at a single gravestone;

we looked at hundred-year-old copper beeches,
    cells burnished purple, soaking up sunshine,

and talked about the dawn redwood,
    how the glimmering light at the beginning

of the world was in all things. This morning,
    in the predawn darkness, Orion angled

in the eastern sky with Sirius, low,
    above the ridgeline; and, before daylight

blotted out the stars, I heard you speak,
    the scratched words return to their sleeves.

Xeriscape

When she hands you a whale vertebra,
you marvel at its heft, at a black

pebble lodged in a lateral nook;
the hollyhocks out the window

stretch into sunshine; a dictionary
in the room is open to *xeriscape;*

the sidewalk and gravel heat all day
and release warmth into the night;

the woman who sits and writes
sees pressed aspen board, framers

setting window headers and door-
jambs—here no polar bears rummage

at the city dump, no seal-oil lamps
flicker in the tide of darkness—

you know the influx of afternoon
clouds, thunder, ball lightning,

wavering lines of rain that evaporate
before they strike the ground,

as you carefully set the whale bone
on the glass table next to the television.

The Far Norway Maples

Silver poplars rise and thin to the very twig,
but what thins at your fingertips?

The aspirations of a minute, a day, a year?
Yellow tangs veer in the water and, catching

sunlight, veer again, disappear from sight.
The unfolding of a life has junctures

that rupture plot: a child folds paper
and glues toothpicks, designs a split-level

house with white walls and pitched roof,
but his father snatches the maquette

and burns it. If you inhale and spore this moment,
it tumors your body, but if you exhale it,

you dissolve midnight and noon; sunlight
tilts and leafs the tips of the far Norway maples.

Sight Lines

I'm walking in sight of the Rio Nambé—

salt cedar rises through silt in an irrigation ditch—

the snowpack in the Sangre de Cristos has already dwindled before spring—

at least no fires erupt in the conifers above Los Alamos—

the plutonium waste has been hauled to an underground site—

a man who built plutonium triggers breeds horses now—

no one could anticipate this distance from Monticello—

Jefferson despised newspapers, but no one thing takes us out of ourselves—

during the Cultural Revolution, a boy saw his mother shot by a firing squad—

a woman detonates when a spam text triggers bombs strapped to her body—

when I come to an upright circular steel lid, I step out of the ditch—

I step out of the ditch but step deeper into myself—

I arrive at a space that no longer needs autumn or spring—

I find ginseng where there is no ginseng my talisman of desire—

though you are visiting Paris, you are here at my fingertips—

though I step back into the ditch, no whitening cloud dispels this world's mystery—

the ditch ran before the year of the Louisiana Purchase—

I'm walking on silt, glimpsing horses in the field—

fielding the shapes of our bodies in white sand—

though parallel lines touch in the infinite, the infinite is here—

The Glass Constellation

Apple branches whiten in moonlight;

no god with an ibis head and human
body writes on a papyrus scroll here;

in daylight, snow has accumulated
on flagstone and fence posts; for days,

masons cut bricks on the patio:

the sound of a circular saw
echoed in your ears, but now scattered

husks of silence lie on the ground;
in a bowl-shaped fountain, water

rises and brims: if all time brims

at this threshold, a man tosses a beer
can out of a car then wrist-flicks a match:

a brush fire ignites, fans east
across a field toward a house and barn;

as the stench of smoke permeates

your clothes and hair, you lean on a shovel:
brush crackles then bursts into flame.

Shoveling snow off a patio, you spot ice
crystals, run your eyes along the glinting—

a varied thrush swallows a juniper berry;

from the air, we track migrating caribou,
and their shifting bodies make visible

the magnetic lines of the moment;
a magpie hops onto an apple-tree stump,

flies to a fence post, up to a branch;

you want that absorption, that vitality
when you turn a key at the door, step inside;

you consider what you've botched:
once you shortened a one-by-eight

so that you could level sand on a portal,

but the foreman stopped and screamed,
"You just sawed off my straightedge!"

Heat waves ripple up from a highway
outside a grapefruit farm near Salton Sea—

the road dissolves into shimmering sand;

you resume shoveling snow off
the walkway and tingle at the hot and cold:

once, in the dark, a large doe stood
behind you—a woman begs outside

the bakery—when he unlatched the gate,

fawns appeared in the orchard—
a temblor torqued the dining room

and silenced the laughter—a spotted towhee
lands on a nest and feeds her fledglings—

gazing into the vortex of the white page:

no jackal-headed god needs to weigh
your heart against an eagle feather—

at sunrise you divert water from the ditch
to sprinklers that swish, spray

the grass—a soldier on point pauses—

who knows the path of a man on crutches
begging at a stoplight?—from the under-

ground uranium mine, a shock wave
shattered windows in the village above—

in the dictionary, you open to *cochlea*

then *pungent*—a thinning membrane,
the earth's atmosphere—you write *respire*

then listen: nibbling dandelion stalks,
a cottontail—as peonies unfold

in a vase, you smell the back of her neck.

Researchers train honeybees, tagged
with microtransmitters, to track TNT

and locate land mines in fields;
Sun Tzu wrote, *to win one hundred*

victories in one hundred battles

is not the acme of skill; in the boiler room,
a plumber replaced a zone valve

but inadvertently let air into the water
line; at midnight, in a house

with no heat, you restart the boiler,

but, on the concrete floor, rat shit
is scattered like rice—though you set

a trap with peanut butter, you recall
a coyote munching an apple core,

gazing through the kitchen window,

unblinking in sunlight; a magpie
lands on a buck and eats ticks;

Sun Tzu wrote, *musical notes are only*
five in number but their melodies

are so numerous one cannot hear them all.

Nasturtium and lobelia planted in pots—
in the silence, a pipa twangs—a cougar

stalks neighborhood dogs in the dark—
you walked up to the acequia

but, finding no water, fingered the silt—

a sniper fires from a second-story window—
fingers start rolling and halting on strings—

where did I put my car keys—I'm ~~pissed~~ late—
what's this ~~fucking~~ note under the door—

behind on my rent?—that sound of a truck

~~coming down the street~~—I need a shot—
not yet—ugh—that sound of glass

breaking—now ~~piss me off~~ I have
to wait until that truck's gone—~~maybe~~

~~I'll move to Denver—~~to back out—

when the caribou arrive, flowering herbs
are starting to wilt—when you type

I have taken too little care—you step
out on a glacial lake at ten below:

ice crystals singe your eyelashes—

you mark the forking branches
of a tree in the darkening air;

minute by minute, your sight shrinks
and shallows until the glass panes

of the door shift from window to mirror;

at that moment, grief and joy tip the ends
of a scale; earlier, you did not know

you would live to see a blue gentian
flower out of air; so often you knew

the page before it burst into flame—

staring at the snowy field of the page,
you tense when an arctic fox

slips past the black trunks of trees:
you blink, and nothing is there;

the blinking cursor marks a pendulum

swinging from a vaulted ceiling
over a marble floor; though no god

fingers your nerves, you write *tingle*
and tingle as sleet turns to rain.

In the white space a poppy buds—

he runs his fingers through her hair—
the spray of mock orange streams by—

at a fountain, a spotted towhee sips—
clenching his hand, he tugs the roots

of her hair—a fisherman unspools a line

back and forth—relaxes his grip—
a fly drops onto a stream, and a cutthroat

snags it—unfolds a sky-blue poppy—
she is rubbing oil on his chest and nipples—

staccato lightning to the west—

swimming in the Pacific, they look
at two lines of dolphins undulating below—

encircling, one suddenly flips
into the air then plunges into the depths—

sound of a car shifting gears—out of PVC

pipes, water gushes into the orchard—
women are rinsing indigo-dyed yarn

in a river—he sees the zigzag blue
lines in tiles above the fireplace as he has

never seen them before—she sees June

light slanting through glass into the hallway—
before his ashes are scattered at sea,

you stare at a dead apricot tree in moonlight:
what was it like to hear a commotion

in the street and glimpse the last emperor

leave the Forbidden City? Years later,
in West Virginia, coal miners, armed

with sticks of dynamite, rolled on cots
into mine openings and then back out—

detonations in the past are laced

in garlic now; sniffing the air
and leaning his head back and forth,

a coyote trots by the glass door;
last night, coyotes howled before

tearing apart a rabbit; at four a.m.

a baker slides dough into an oven:
the aroma rises from the basement kiln—

and, as you inhale, it drizzles on deck:
three miles from the coastline,

you scattered ashes, and swirling

on waves, they formed a gray,
black-speckled cloud before sinking—

at the beach, you screwed
an umbrella pole into the sand,

heard cry and cry but saw nothing:

then a piping plover, skirting
toward the water, revealed,

behind rocks, four speckled eggs;
after replanting the pole, sitting under

an umbrella, you felt how a skin

separated you from death, how death
contoured the pause between exhale

and inhale, how it flowered inside
the bougainvillea blooming by a glass

door and sparked the white page

into light; and, as glass molecules
slow as the temperature cools

yet never lock into crystal patterns,
you feel how *once* never locks,

how it vibrates, quickens inside you:

then you level with a taxi driver
swerving between trucks, level

with a potter who mashes a bowl
back into a ball, level with a magpie

that congregates and squawks

with other magpies over a corpse
before flying off, and when you hike

up the ridge, dew rising into
the morning, you ride the flex

of your muscles as you lift the gate—

The White Orchard

NEW POEMS

Circumference

Vanilla farmers in Madagascar sit in the dark with rifles;
at two a.m., after a thunderstorm,

I lurch down the hallway to check the oak floor
under a skylight, place a towel

in a pan. As if armed, waiting for a blue string
to trip a thief, I listen

in the hush at a point where ink flows out of a pen
onto a white Sahara of a page.

Adjusting the rearview mirror in the car before backing
out of the garage, I ask, What

is the logarithm of a dream? How do you trace a sphere
whose center is nowhere?

It is hard to believe farmers pollinate vanilla orchids
with toothpick-sized needles,

yet we do as needed; pouring syrup on a pancake,
I catch the scent of vines,

race along the circumference, sensing what it's like to sit
in the dark with nothing in my hands.

Entanglement

1

Before sunrise, you listen for deer beyond
the gate: no signs of turkeys roosting on branches,
no black bear overturning garbage bins
along the street. The day glimmers
like waves undulating with the tide:
you toss another yellow cedar log
into the woodstove on the float house;
a great blue heron flaps its wings,
settles on the railing outside the window;
a thin low cloud of smoke hangs over the bay.
When you least expect it, your field
of vision tears, and an underlying landscape
reveals a radiating moment in time.
Today you put aside the newspaper,
soak strawberry plants in a garden bed;
yet, standing on land, you feel the rise
and fall of a float house, how the earth
under your feet is not fixed but moves with the tide.

2

Searching for lightning petroglyphs, I stumble
on a rattlesnake skin between rocks—

at dusk, soldiers set up machine guns
near the entrance to the Taj; others lay

a wall of sandbags—and tense when
a snake glides past my feet—a cow

lumbers through a crowded street,
while a one-armed girl panhandles

at a blinking red light—relax when
a tail without rattles slips into a crevice—

a vendor sells dates and mangoes; my eyes
sting in the soot-laden cardamom air—

when I stop at a pair of zigzag petroglyphs
and ponder if they are lightning or snakes,

I look up at a sandstone temple with chariots
and war elephants carved in the first tier;

above, a naked woman pulls a thorn from her heel;
higher up, a man and woman entwine.

3

You pick grapes from a street vendor
when an ambulance packed with explosives
detonates in a crowd; while I was weeding
in the garden, a fire ant crawled up my jeans
and blistered my leg. I gaze at the white trunks
of aspens and shrinking patches of snow
on the grass; no one can read the script
of Rongorongo, yet we know the urge to carve
with a shark's tooth. The warmth of sunlight
radiates from a stone wall: a wall formed
of hewed words, fitted without mortar—
piano music wafted like frankincense smoke—
each word, a meteor leaving a track.
The shift from opacity to transparency's
a form of sunrise; at five a.m. you step outside
and absorb a lunar eclipse; I recall patches
of moonlight rippling down the hallway;
now we are X, collapsing space, collapsing time.

4

Our bodies by firelight—

apple blossoms unfolding at the tips of branches—

aroma of candlelight in the room—

spruce trees, black, against a lightening sky—

leafing willow swaying in the backyard—

a moment of red tulips—

navel-orange slices on a plate—

squares of dark chocolate—

eddies in a river—

a sword razors a leaf coming downstream—

a dog leaps between slats of a fence—

rips a gate off its hinges—

ring, ring, ring, ring, ring—

scent of blackthorn oil—

these rings we've worn and worn into sunrise—

5

Along the shore, bald eagles nest in the yellow cedars—

my clothes reek of cedar smoke—

I wrap clothes around glass jars of king salmon in my knapsack—

standing on a dock, I board a floatplane—

floaters in my eyes, wherever I go—

wherever you go, you cannot travel faster than light—

synapses firing in my body are a form of light—

threads of fugitive dye entangled in neural firings—

scent of summer in the blackening leaves—

a black bear swipes a screen door and ransacks a kitchen—

we ransack the past and discover action at a distance—

entangled waves of near and far—

a photon fired through a slit behaves like a wave—

we inhale, and our lungs oxygenate a cosmos—

a fire breaks out of the secret depths of the earth—

revel in the beauty of form.

6

A ring-necked pheasant forages along the road,
while a purple orchid blooms by the window;
when distance collapses, a bloodred
strawberry bursts in your mouth;
you mark the rise and fall of your lungs,
blood coursing to your fingertips and toes;
when you consider gasoline mixed with seawater,
a torch flares out of the past into present:
you dip your brush in the ink of existence
and daub words that blacken, burst into flame—
a child in a boat gnaws stale bread.
Standing in an orchard, listening, aching
at the stars, I hear water drip off
stalactites and splash onto a cavern floor;
by daylight, the apple trees are covered
with blossoms; yet, now, in the dark,
I experience a wave of moonlight
glittering sheets of thin ice bobbing out in the bay.

Eye Exam

E D F C Z P
his eyesight is tethered to shore—

no sign of zebras
but spotted towhees repair their nest;

before the ditch is cleared,
plum trees are blossoming along a riparian bank—

he pauses at the gaps between letters,
notices how his mind has an urge to wander,

how it resists being tethered to question and quick reply—
yellow daffodils are rising in the yard;

behind his eyelids,
a surge of aquamarine water is breaking to shore:

they are stretching,
they are contorting into bliss—

and as the ophthalmologist
rotates lenses, "Is it clearer with 1 or 2?"

he sees how this moment is lens, mirror, spring,
and how, "1,"

D E F P O T E C
sharpens his vision to this o, the earth.

Pitch Blue

I can't stop—

Wading into a lake—

Skipping one flat stone after another across the surface of a pond—

In a sarcophagus,
lapis inlaid along the eyelids of a death mask—

Wool oxidizing when pulled out of the dye bath—

Like a deserted village with men approaching on horseback—

The moment before collision—

Never light this match—

La Cieneguilla

Today no men shout from the cave and toss beer cans—
meandering along the cliff face, you find
a cluster of petroglyphs: in a procession,
five humpbacked flute players, a dragonfly,
turkey, star—or is it compass?—antelope,
great blue heron with a fish in its beak.

A kestrel glides overhead; glancing
below at a bare marsh, you notice
a desiccation to this site—when you pulled
up to a gas pump on Sunday morning,
a woman in a pickup raced alongside
and demanded money, "I need a tank of gas

to get to Phoenix, no, Las Vegas, *Las Vegas*—"
and she leaned as if to raise a pistol
to the open window. When you shook
your head, she tore out of the station,
careened down the road. Staring
at a lightning petroglyph, you mark

the zigzag beauty of danger, and how
hunger animates our nights and days;
you visualize corn planted in a sloping arroyo,
green shoots rising after rain, and nod
at the zigzag danger of beauty, then
walk from this site, this point of no—and infinite—return.

Ravine

Stopping to catch my breath on a switchback,
I run my fingers along the leaves of a yucca:

each blade curved, sharp, radiating from a core—
in this warmest of Novembers, the dead

push out of thawing permafrost: in a huge
blotch of black ink that hangs, framed,

on a wall, Gu Cheng wrote the character
fate, and a woman shrugs, *"When you look*

at me, you're far away." Last night, gazing
at Orion's belt and sword sparkling in the sky,

I saw how we yearn for connection where
no connection exists: what belt, what sword?

Glancing at boulders in the ravine, I catch
a flock of Steller's jays scavenging along

the ground; I scavenge among pine needles
for one to breathe into flame, gaze

at yuccas whose blades collect dew at dawn
and at dust floating in sunlight above the trail.

October Dusk

Aspen leaves and blue spruce needles dissolve
in the dusk; looking through glass panes,
you see ceiling lights, a Bolivian
textile on a wall: when what's behind becomes
what's in front, you wince, draw circles,
and, deepening the graphite tracks on a page,
enact a noose; then a sliver of moon
in the sky's a sickle; a twig fire crackles
at your feet; you whistle, ache, step
out of a car to find bits of shattered glass
on asphalt resemble the ends of dreams;
as you flip bottles into a recycling bin,
each glass shatters: each dream collapses
into a pile of shards; as you toss the last
glass into the bin, you step out of another
transparent confine; and, as moonlight makes
a road on water, you have no word for
this moment that rides a wave stilling all waves.

Midnight Flame

At midnight, he can't see
        the white picket fence
                or the tomato stalks, shriveled,

in the garden, though
        he knows the patio,
                strewn with willow leaves,

plumes of tall grasses,
        upright and still;
                and, as he peers into the yard,

he senses a moment
        wicking into flame—
                walking up an arroyo,

they gaze back
        across the Pojoaque valley,
                spot the glinting tin roofs,

cottonwoods leafing
        along the curves of the river—
                a green tide

surges in their arteries
        as well as the trees;
                tonight, spring infuses fall,

and memory's wick
        draws the liquefied
                wax of experience up into flame.

Festina lente

Ping. ping, ping—

            I hear nailing across the street and suddenly recall,
in my hands, nailing rebar

                        through two corbels angled over a post;

            after a night of rain,
a young swallowtail sips nectar at a purple flower;

I sip the morning sunrise,
            glimpse a trogon between ovate leaves,
                                    a keel-billed toucan on a branch—

on a portal, a neighbor had six hummingbird feeders;
            when I tried to discuss the ditch and times for watering,

            while a rufous darted from feeder to feeder,

the humming from black-chinned hummingbirds
                        thrummed out his words;

now I find moments of the past ring like tuning forks—

I follow the tide of my breath
            and, in the shoals of daylight,

                        begin to, *festina lente,* move,
as a series of concentric circles moves out, over the surface of water,

into a life that synaptically connects the shimmer of a leaf,
my hand in your hair, your hand

            on my shoulder, an afternoon thunderstorm
                                    gathering from the west,

                        as we situate at the brink of this wild-eyed world—

Pitch Yellow

Peony leaf dropping to earth—

A scorpion in amber—

Gluing pieces of a three-masted ship while listening to boxing on the radio—

Gold sieved out of reverie—

Threads, plucked from crocus flowers and dried—

A lit fuse igniting a firework—

Chromium, cobalt, copper particulates downstream—

Crawl, scrape, stagger, stagger out: spelunker—

Be X blossoming into song—

Sleepers

A black-chinned hummingbird lands
on a metal wire and rests for five seconds;
for five seconds, a pianist lowers his head
and rests his hands on the keys;

a man bathes where irrigation water
forms a pool before it drains into the river;
a mechanic untwists a plug, and engine oil
drains into a bucket; for five seconds,

I smell peppermint through an open window,
recall where a wild leaf grazed your skin;
here touch comes before sight; holding you,
I recall, across a canal, the sounds of men

laying cuttlefish on ice at first light;
before first light, physical contact,
our hearts beating, patter of female rain
on the roof; as the hummingbird

whirs out of sight, the gears of a clock
mesh at varying speeds; we hear
a series of ostinato notes and are not tied
to our bodies' weight on earth.

Earthrise

Zoom in to pink bougainvillea in an iron-
        glazed pot, along the edge of a still pool;

beyond tiled roofs below, surf crashes
        against black lava rock; palm fronds

ripple in the air. Miners in an open pit
        slog through sludge, panning for gold;

when they find a nugget, a foreman
        seizes it; is there endless mire

and exploitation from a patch of ground?
        In a wheelchair, an eighty-year-old man

proclaims, "Go in and hit them hard."
        Hit whom hard? From the air, a coastline

dotted with golf courses and sand traps,
        whitecapping surf, a cloud forest,

five volcanoes rising out of the ocean,
        a shrinking island, earthrise from the moon.

Acequia del Llano

1

The word *acequia* is derived from the Arabic *as-saqiya* (water conduit) and refers to an irrigation ditch that transports water from a river to farms and fields, as well as the association of members connected to it.

Blossoming peach trees—
to the west, steel buildings glint
above the mesa.

In Santa Fe, New Mexico, the Acequia del Llano is one and a half miles long and begins at Nichols Reservoir dam. At the bottom of the dam, an outlet structure and flow meter control water that runs through a four-inch pipe at up to one hundred fifty gallons per minute. The water runs along a hillside and eventually drops into the Santa Fe River. Fifteen families and two organizations belong to this ditch association, and the acequia irrigates about thirty acres of gardens and orchards.

In the ditch, water flowing—
now an eagle-feather wind.

2

Yarrow, rabbitbrush, claret cup cactus, one-seed juniper, Douglas fir, and scarlet penstemon are some of the plants in this environment. Endangered and threatened species include the southwestern willow flycatcher, the least tern, the violet-crowned hummingbird, the American marten, and the white-tailed ptarmigan.

Turning my flashlight
behind me, I see a large
buck, three feet away.

Each April, all of the members come, or hire workers who come, to do the annual spring cleaning; this involves walking the length of the ditch, using shovels and clippers to clear branches, silt, and other debris.

Twigs, pine needles, plastic bags
cleared today before moonrise—

3

The ditch association is organized with a *mayordomo,* ditch manager, who oversees the distribution of water according to each *parciante*'s (holder of water rights) allotment. The acequia runs at a higher elevation than all of the land held by the *parciantes,* so the flow of water is gravity fed.

Crisscrossing the ditch,
avoiding cholla,
I snag my hair on branches.

Each year the irrigation season runs from about April 15 to October 15. On Thursdays and Sundays, at 5:30 a.m., I get up and walk about a quarter of a mile uphill to the ditch and drop a metal gate into it. When the water level rises, water goes through screens then down two pipes and runs below to irrigate grass, lilacs, trees, and an orchard.

Across the valley, ten lights
glimmer from hillside houses.

4

Orion and other constellations of stars stand out at that hour. As it moves toward summer, the constellations shift, and, by July 1, when I walk uphill, I walk in early daylight. By mid-September, I again go uphill in the dark and listen for coyote and deer in between the piñons and junipers.

One by one, we light
candles on leaves, let them go
flickering downstream.

The Ganges River is 1,569 miles long. The Rio Grande is 1,896 miles long; it periodically dries up, but when it runs its full length, it runs from its headwaters in the mountains of southern Colorado into the Gulf of Mexico. Water from the Santa Fe River runs into the Rio Grande. Water from the Acequia del Llano runs into the Santa Fe River. From a length of one hundred paces along the acequia, I draw our allotment of water.

Here, I pull a translucent
cactus spine out of your hand.

Pyrocumulus

Peony shoots rise out of the earth;
at five a.m., walking up the ridge,
I mark how, in April, Orion's left arm
was an apex in the sky, and, by May,
only Venus flickered above the ridge
against the blue edge of sunrise.
In daylight, a pear tree explodes
with white blossoms—no black-
footed ferret slips across my path,
no boreal owl stirs on a branch.
At three a.m., dogs seethed and howled
when a black bear snagged a shriveled
apple off a branch; and, waking out
of a black pool, I glimpsed how
fire creates its own weather
in rising pyrocumulus. Reaching
the ditch, I drop the gate: it's time
for the downhill pipes to fill,
time for bamboo at the house
to suck up water, time to see sunlight
flare between leaves before
the scorching edge of afternoon.

Midnight Spark

A rotating convective column of flames
pulls a cloud of hot smoke 10,000 feet high;

until July 1, the precipitation was 1.25

inches for the year; a few young cottonwoods
along the river have dropped leaves;

wherever you go, you recall yellow tape

and police cars at a gas station; driving past
Kewa Pueblo, you visualize drummers

shifting direction, and, in the realignment,

dancers momentarily pause then step
with the sounds of gourds enacting rain;

approaching La Cienega, you know a wind

capable of bending steel pipes around trees;
and, in the dark, passing cars pulled off the highway,

you no longer see lights and rain but spark

at the gap between lightning and thunder,
a free fall before the cusp of dawn.

Whiteout

Honey mushrooms glow in the dark;
in a sweat, a journalist wakes

to a roadside bomb; when a woman
outside a bakery offers to wash

your car windshield, you give her
some cash, and what will suffice?

Cottonwood seeds swirl in the air;
in Medellín, your host invites you

to lunch at his house; you sip
potato and cilantro soup, glance

at a door open to an enclosed yard
with a hammock and mango tree,

the space a refuge inside bullet-
pocked walls. A narwhal pokes

its tusk through ice into the air;
it exhales: whiteout: *how to live,*

where to go: in the yard, you hear
a circular saw rip the length of a plank.

Invisible Globe

Hiking up a trail in the snow, I spot
the rusting orange body of a car;

in midwinter, the sun's a mirage
of July—a woman begins Taiji

movements and rotates an invisible
globe; a sky-blue morning glory

unfolds on a fence; though
the movements appear to be stretches,

they contain the tips of deflections
and strikes; behind a fence, neighbors

drink beer, grill chicken, laugh—
as snowflakes drop, I guess at

their shapes: *twelve-branched,*
stellar dendrite, triangular, capped

column—under a ceiling fan,
I recall our hours in a curtained

room—and as I sidestep down,
a *capped column* dissolves on my face.

Pitch Magenta

A broad-tailed hummingbird sips at a penstemon—

Plunging off a cliff face into an abyss—

Wiping a deer tail across cactus, he collects cochineal bugs in a pan—

When she tugs and bites his lower lip—

Like a fire truck hurtling through traffic—

Embalming a chameleon with coriander seeds,
stitching it closed with silk, placing it on his right shoulder—

Rising notes of a siren as an ambulance passes—

Surge in their bodies, pupils dilated—

The White Orchard

Under a supermoon, you gaze into the orchard—

a glassblower shapes a glowing orange mass into a horse—

you step into a space where you once lived—

crushed mica glitters on plastered walls—

a raccoon strolls in moonlight along the top of an adobe wall—

swimming in a pond, we notice a reflected cottonwood on the water—

clang: a deer leaps over the gate—

every fifteen minutes an elephant is shot for its tusks—

you mark a bleached earless lizard against the snowfall of this white page—

the skins of eggplants glistening in a garden—

our bodies glistening by firelight—

though skunks once ravaged corn, our bright moments cannot be ravaged—

sleeping near a canal, you hear lapping waves—

at dawn, waves lapping and the noise of men unloading scallops and shrimp—

no noise of gunshots—

you focus on the branches of hundred-year-old apple trees—

opening the door, we find red and yellow rose petals scattered on our bed—

then light-years—

you see pear branches farther in the orchard as the moon rises—

branches bending under the snow of this white page—

Rock Paper Scissors

Midnight snow swirls in the courtyard—
you wake and mark the steel-gray light of dawn,

the rhythm in your hands
of scissors cutting paper;

you pull a blade against ribbon,
and the ribbon springs into a spiraling curl
when you release it;

here, one pulled a blade against the ribbon of desire,
a downy woodpecker drilled into a desiccated pear tree—

you consider how paper wraps rock,
scissors snips paper,

how this game embodies the evolution
of bacteria and antibiotic;

you can't see your fingerprints on a door handle,
but your smudging,

like trudging footprints in snow,

tracks where and how you go

wrapping
a chrysoprase heart in a box—

how you look at a series of incidentals
and pull an invisible thread through them all.

Trawler

In first light, a raucous, repeating cry of a bird—
you squint at the ocean, where the edge
of far water, darker than sky, limns

the curving horizon; a white trawler
inches along the coast, and white specks
of other times appear—bobbing

in waves that break behind you and roll
onto a Kilauea beach; a mushroom
rises below a palm tree, unfolds

a convex cap: the cap flattens and releases
spores into the air—waves of pleasure
run through your body and hers;

in early light, you bathe at an outdoor shower:
shadows of palm leaves against a wall,
a single plumeria blossom on a tree—

and, wherever you are, the moon
pulls in waves breaking
and receding, breaking and receding along a coast.

Morning Islands

Squinting across the water at another island
formed by volcanoes above the ocean,

I hike into and across a crater, stop
at silverswords—palm leaves rustle

in the breeze, and what prognostication
is that for today? In moonlight,

a mongoose darts across our headlights:
we drive along another island's

coast to the ranch at a lava road's end;
wandering among boulders and streams,

I slip on a rock, midstream; sipping
kava from wooden bowls, we gaze

at surf below the cliff—I dive
without diving, standing in a *Wuji*

stance, inhaling as my hands rise
above my head, exhaling as they move down.

Blackcap

V E R G E:
she sets type by hand and loves how the spaces

between letters and between words
are of the same type-metal the letters themselves are cast from:

o p e n   w a t e r:
standing along the Malecón, I gaze at the curving horizon of water and sky,
at whitecaps crashing below;

now, walking barefoot on an oak floor,

I expect to see, through the glass panes,
a stag enter the moonlit orchard

where autumn hangs in the branches, like smoked bourbon,
but no, not yet:

to arrive at a place where each letter of each word
rises out of metallic silence,

and in the yearning for this language to blackcap,
I ride a hush, a wave

where the silence will be broken,
when dogs bark at whatever crosses the fence line.

Cloud Forest

Against the mountain slope, incoming fog—

we stood near the maroon strips of bark and inhaled the aroma of a rainbow eucalyptus—

in the Netherlands, a rising sea-level is stressing dikes—

an ʻakepa is singing—

waves were whitecapping against black lava rock—

on an atoll, nuclear waste was dumped into a concrete vault—

we find these truths to be self-evident—

in a past life, I played the clarinet in a marching band—

now the vault has cracked—

have we not meandered, bewildered, in a cloud forest?—

along this coast, you are tracing the contours of desire—

the pilot veers the helicopter up over the canyon rim as we gasp—

the ʻāmaui has vanished—

we step into red-ginger daylight—

The Open Water

1

Peaches redden on branches; in the dark,
I drop the irrigation gate—each month

a woman crosses Havana Bay and, looking

at the open water, reclaims her mother—
I smell the bloodred strawberries

in the garden; at a flaking green tank,

I listen: yellow light shines at a neighbor's
octagonal window; Orion dims as the sky lightens—

what am I but a wandering speck

rambling, smudging, stumbling, writing—
someone opens a car door and steals quarters—

across the valley, two lights flicker from houses;

standing before a sharp descent, I look
at a waxing moon—the big bang's

always present—I latch a green metal

gate near the empty stable and smell
your neck as you turn in your sleep;

daylight reaches the porch post columns;

I open a glass door and sit at a table,
where light pools onto the wood floor.

2

A black butterfly opens its wings—

sitting in a bus on a metal seat, I notice the steel above the driver has corroded, and
pinpricks of daylight stream through—

two destroyers moored offshore—

on a scaffold, he uses a roller and paints the building marine blue—

a mime in a silver top hat, silver jacket—hands and face, silvered—inches through
a restaurant—

standing in the shade looking up into the branches and leaves of a thorned ceiba tree—

a street sweeper emigrates and founds a chain of restaurants—

two men push pig carcasses on a cart through the doorway—

a singer shaking maracas sways to the music—

3

Russian sage scents the air—

the aroma of flickering candles
on the fireplace mantel—

that I am even here standing on a ridge looking at Venus low in the sky—

a black bear overturns a dumpster in the garage
and eats remnants
of a chicken enchilada—

soldiers move through the airport with dogs on leashes—

I rub oil on your breasts—

in Old Delhi, uncovered bins with saffron, cardamom,
ginger, turmeric—

a poster warns of an imminent terrorist attack—

I jot things down so that when I lose them in the darkness
I may recover them quickly with the dawn—

dancers emerge wearing Yoruba masks—

I taste the salt on your neck—

that the rivers of the world flow into the seas—

that I am alive and hear rotating sprinklers jet water onto the grass—

that we go through the day humming in our bodies—

Russian sage emerges out of darkness—

4

In August sunlight, basil plants go to seed—
a mime dressed as a construction worker

with gold skin, gold goggles, helmet,
and sledgehammer, stands in the shady

side of a cobbled street; when you drop
some cash in the box, he smiles and bows—

a woman gives you a book of poetry;
when you read *la pobreza del lugar,*

you bristle: no place is impoverished
if the mind sparks; if not, the dunes

of a Sahara have no end; the sun sets,
and a cooling range is under the stars—

when the mind seeds, a camel emerges
out of a dune and you ride it to an oasis,

where you imbibe ayahuasca: up all night,
when the man leading the vigil puts on

a jaguar mask and becomes a jaguar,
you raise your hands, and they spark butterflies.

5

A singer shaking maracas sways to the music—

in the street, a Black man pushing a cart with strings of onions dangling from the frame sings, "Onions for sale"—

a girl with silvered face and hands, blouse and skirt, holds a silver bouquet of flowers—

a purple 1953 Chevy with polished chrome parked alongside an azure Bonneville—

in the yard, a flowering boojum tree—

his mother's father was the owner of a sugar plantation and disinherited his mother after she married a mulatto street sweeper—

sitting in the oven of a bus—

a mime dressed as a deep-sea diver, helmet in hand, inches up the stairs—

a black butterfly closes its wings—

6

Clusters of conical thorns on the tree trunk—
I recall screech owls perched on a post
protected from sunlight by wisteria leaves,
the hush in the courtyard during a snowfall,
cinders from a forest fire alighting on
the roof, and how winter starlight shifted
to summer sunshine within a single day.
In the eyehook between shelves, I see
the upright primary wing feather of an eagle,
the red and orange bougainvilleas,
entwined, rising from a pot pressing
against the ceiling and against glass doors;
twice I stepped on lye-softened floorboards
and caught splinters. I mark presence
in absence and absence in presence:
as a May snow landing on a walkway
dissolves as it lands, as surf rises
and sweeps across the plazas and boulevards.

Transpirations

Leafing branches of a backyard plum—

branches of water on a dissolving ice sheet—

chatter of magpies when you approach—

lilacs lean over the road, weighted with purple blossoms—

then the noon sun shimmers the grasses—

you ride the surge into summer—

smell of piñon crackling in the fireplace—

blued notes of a saxophone in the air—

not by sand running through an hourglass but by our bodies igniting—

passing in the form of vapors from a living body—

this world of orange sunlight and wildfire haze—

world of iron filings pulled toward magnetic south and north—

pool of quicksilver when you bend to tie your shoes—

standing, you well up with glistening eyes—

have you lived with utmost care?—

have you articulated emotions like the edges of leaves?—

adjusting your breath to the seasonal rhythm of grasses—

gazing into a lake on a salt flat and drinking, in reflection, the Milky Way—

Acknowledgments

Grateful acknowledgment is made to the editors of the following publications in which the New Poems, sometimes in earlier versions, first appeared:

Academy of American Poets Poem-a-Day (Poets.org): "Rock Paper Scissors," "Sleepers"
Big Other: "Blackcap"
Conjunctions: "The Open Water"
FIELD: "La Cieneguilla," "Pitch Blue"
Harvard Review: "Morning Islands"
Kenyon Review: "Acequia del Llano," "Eye Exam," "Pyrocumulus," "Trawler," "The White Orchard," "Whiteout"
Lana Turner: "Festina lente," "Pitch Magenta," "Pitch Yellow"
Los Angeles Review of Books: "October Dusk"
The Massachusetts Review: "Ravine"
New England Review: "Entanglement"
The New Republic: "Cloud Forest"
The New Yorker: "Transpirations"
Plume (online): "Circumference," "Earthrise"
Poetry: "Midnight Flame"
Reed Magazine: "Midnight Spark"
Tin House: "Invisible Globe"

"The White Orchard" appeared in *The Best American Poetry 2019* (Scribner, 2019) and also in the *2020 Pushcart Prize XLIV: Best of the Small Presses* (Pushcart Press, 2019).

Twelve poems, in three groupings of four poems—"First Snow," "Invisible Globe," "Eye Exam," "Unpacking a Globe"; "Sleepers," "Light Echoes," "Ravine," "Black Center"; "La Cieneguilla," "Traversal," "The White Orchard," "Courtyard Fire"—were published as a limited edition letterpress chapbook, *Starlight Behind Daylight* (St Brigid Press, 2020).

The following ten books of poetry were first published as listed below:
The Willow Wind (Rainbow Zenith Press, 1972; revised, Tooth of Time Books, 1981)
Two Ravens (Tooth of Time Books, 1976; revised, Tooth of Time Books, 1984)
Dazzled (Floating Island Publications, 1982)
River River (Lost Roads Publishers, 1987)

Archipelago (Copper Canyon Press, 1995)
The Redshifting Web: Poems 1970–1998 (Copper Canyon Press, 1998)
Quipu (Copper Canyon Press, 2005)
The Ginkgo Light (Copper Canyon Press, 2009)
Compass Rose (Copper Canyon Press, 2014)
Sight Lines (Copper Canyon Press, 2019)

Thank you Mei-mei Berssenbrugge, Carol Moldaw, Dana Levin, and Jim Moore, for close readings of these poems.

Thank you, Michael Wiegers, for your unflagging support of my work through the years.

Notes

The poems in this collection span fifty years. I have decided to retain the spellings of Chinese names in the forms used when the poems were first published, so Wade-Giles and pinyin romanizations both appear, though there's a clear tendency to use pinyin over time. Page numbers indicate the first occurrence.

p. 10 Man On Horseback: the *Tricholoma flavovirens* mushroom.

p. 10 s twist, z twist: threads of fiber may be spun in either an s-spin (counterclockwise) or z-spin (clockwise) direction.

p. 13 A catalogue of endangered species.

p. 18 *kaiseki:* (Japanese) breast stones; an intricate, multicourse Zen meal that accompanies tea ceremony.

p. 18 Qianlong: Chinese emperor from 1736 to 1799.

p. 19 Daruma: (Japanese) Bodhidharma, the founder of Zen.

p. 21 Tokpela: (Hopi) sky, the name of the first world.

p. 21 *trastero:* in the Southwest, a cupboard.

p. 23 feng shui: (Chinese) wind and water; the art of balancing and enhancing the environment.

p. 23 Two Grey Hills: a style of Navajo weaving that uses undyed wool in intricate patterns.

p. 26 *matcha:* (Japanese) a powdered green tea.

p. 30 *kukui:* Hawaiian name for the candlenut tree.

p. 35 *huan wo he shan:* (Chinese) return my rivers and mountains.

p. 37 *ʻapapane, ʻiʻiwi:* names of Hawaiian birds.

p. 40 *oʻo aʻa:* extinct Hawaiian bird.

p. 76 *ristras:* in the Southwest, strings of dried red chiles.

p. 87 *canal:* a waterspout off a roof.

p. 87 *vigas:* ceiling beams.

p. 87 *latillas:* stripped aspen poles laid across ceiling beams.

p. 94 Questa: a village in Northern New Mexico.

p. 149 *Koyemsi:* mudhead kachinas, clowns that serve religious and secular functions at Hopi ceremonies.

p. 159 *Kwakwha*: (Hopi) thank you (*masc*).

p. 159 *Askwali:* (Hopi) thank you (*fem*).

p. 170 *enso:* in Zen calligraphy, the circle.

p. 176 *shibui:* (Japanese) astringent, refined; a Zen aesthetic that finds beauty in restraint and in the unassuming.

p. 177 *karez:* irrigation tunnels.

p. 188 The setting for this poem is Sanjusangendo in Kyoto. Thanks to Ken Rodgers for verifying the spatial orientation at this temple.

p. 189 *chacmool:* (Mayan) a reclining human figure with flexed knees, head turned to the side, hands holding a basin at the navel.

p. 198 erhu: a Chinese two-stringed musical instrument held in the lap and played with a bow.

p. 198 piki: (Hopi) an extremely fragile, paper-thin bread made from blue cornmeal.

p. 203 TLV: in the Han dynasty, a series of so-called TLV mirrors appeared; the backs of these mirrors have geomantic forms resembling the letters *T, L, V.*

p. 205 *xuan:* the Chinese character means dark, deep, profound, subtle and is etymologically derived from dyeing.

p. 215 *traduttori, traditori:* (Italian) translators are traitors.

p. 227 *blak, blæc:* the Middle English and Old English spellings of *black;* they are homophones with the word *black.*

p. 231 quipu: Although quipus are usually thought of in connection with the Incas, ancient quipus exist in Asian cultures as well. In China, one can use the phrase *chieh shêng chi shih,* which means "the memorandum or record of knotted cords," to refer to how Chinese writing evolved before characters were invented.

p. 232 *Lepiota naucina:* a mushroom that appears in grass and marks the beginning of autumn.

p. 234 earthshine: sunlight reflected by the earth that illuminates the dark part of the moon.

p. 244 omega minus: a subatomic particle predicted by Murray Gell-Mann in 1962 and verified two years later.

p. 246 *jarana:* in Mexico, a small folk guitar.

p. 266 *genmai:* (Japanese) a combination of green tea and roasted popped brown rice.

p. 271 *Bombyx mori:* silkworm.

p. 274 Coal Sack: a dark patch of obscuring dust in the far southern Milky Way.

p. 279 raki: (Turkish) an aniseed liqueur, which, with water, turns milky white.

p. 280 *granero:* in the Southwest, a granary container.

p. 283 Lingzhi: (Chinese) a mushroom that is reputed to provide health and longevity, the "mushroom of immortality."

p. 288 *dhyāna:* (Sanskrit) a fixed state of contemplation.

p. 294 Didyma: the site of a Greek oracular sanctuary in Asia Minor that includes the remains of a Temple of Apollo.

p. 301 Çanakkale: the principal town, situated on the Asian side, at the narrowest point of the strait between Europe and Asia.

p. 303 Black Trumpets: *Craterellus fallax,* edible funnel-shaped mushrooms.

p. 317 *xun:* (Chinese) a globular ceramic-vessel flute with holes.

p. 348 Teec Nos Pos: a style of Navajo weaving that uses wide borders featuring geometric elements around a center of bold abstract design.

p. 353 yardangs: desert landforms that usually occur in groups; they are narrow, steep-sided ridges carved into bedrock, with the ridges running parallel to one another and in the direction of the prevailing wind.

p. 353 *ciénega:* (Spanish) swamp or marsh.

p. 353 Tsé Bit'a'í: (Diné) the rock with wings; Shiprock, located in northwestern New Mexico.

p. 360 Yerba mansa is a perennial flowering plant (*Anemopsis californica*). In New Mexico, people boil the roots to make a medicinal tea.

p. 370 This boathouse in Laugharne, Wales, is where Dylan Thomas lived, and the house is set in a cliff overlooking the Taf Estuary.

p. 370 I first heard that *å i åa ä e ö,* in Swedish, means *island in the river* from the Dutch poet K. Michel. The Norwegian writer Dag Straumsvåg sourced this all-vowel sentence to Swedish poet Gustaf Fröding's "Dumt Fôlk" (Stupid People). Thanks to David Caligiuri and Connie Wanek.

p. 372 A sarangi is a short-necked string instrument of India. Of all the East Indian instruments, it is said to most resemble the sound of the human voice.

p. 394 A leograph is a mythical lion figure.

p. 412 "The Unfolding Center" is also the name of my collaboration with sculptor Susan York, where Susan made twenty-two graphite drawings that accompany this poem.

p. 412 *Green snail spring* (*Bi Luo Chun*) is a green tea that comes from the Dong Ting mountain region in Jiangsu, China. Picked in early spring, the leaves are rolled into a tight spiral and resemble snail meat.

p. 422 "Flip a house and it's shelter" and the following three lines are based on an interview with Santa Fe architect Trey Jordan.

p. 425 "Water Calligraphy" (*dì shū*): at sunrise in China, elderly men often go to public parks, dip brushes in water, and write calligraphy on the slate walkways. As the water evaporates, the characters disappear.

p. 436 "Cloud Hands" is for JoAnna Schoon.

p. 456 In "Courtyard Fire," the italicized lines are a condensation of a sentence from Karl Marx's "A Contribution to the Critique of Hegel's *Philosophy of Right*" (1884).

p. 463 *kintsugi:* (Japanese) golden joinery, the art of repairing broken pottery with gold-dusted lacquer.

p. 466 *This is the writing, the speaking of the dream* is Dennis Tedlock's translation of the beginning of a series of glyphs on a Mayan ceramic vessel.

p. 471 "Dawn Redwood" is in memory of C.D. Wright. The italicized line is from her poem "Floating Trees."

p. 477–8 The italicized lines are from *The Art of War* by Sun Tzu, translated by Samuel B. Griffith (New York: Oxford University Press, 1963).

p. 512 *Wuji,* sometimes called the Emptiness posture, is a warm-up position in Taiji and Qigong practices.

p. 513 Malecón: a seawall that stretches for five miles along the coast in Havana, Cuba.

p. 514 ʻakepa: a small, brightly colored Hawaiian honeycreeper.

p. 514 ʻāmaui: extinct Hawaiian bird.

p. 518 *la pobreza del lugar:* (Spanish) the poverty of the place; from "Voy a Nombrar Las Cosas" ("I Am Going to Name the Things") by Eliseo Diego.

About the Author

Arthur Sze is a poet, translator, and editor. He is the author of eleven books of poetry, including *Sight Lines* (2019), for which he received the National Book Award; *Compass Rose* (2014), a Pulitzer Prize finalist; *The Ginkgo Light* (2009), selected for the PEN Southwest Book Award and the Mountains & Plains Independent Booksellers Association Book Award; *Quipu* (2005); *The Redshifting Web: Poems 1970–1998* (1998), selected for the Balcones Poetry Prize and the Asian American Literary Award; and *Archipelago* (1995), selected for an American Book Award. He has also published one book of Chinese poetry translations, *The Silk Dragon* (2001), selected for the Western States Book Award, and edited *Chinese Writers on Writing* (2010). A recipient of the eighth annual 'T' Space Poetry Award, the Jackson Poetry Prize from Poets & Writers, a Lannan Literary Award, a Guggenheim Fellowship, a Lila Wallace–Reader's Digest Writers' Award, two National Endowment for the Arts Creative Writing Fellowships, a Howard Foundation Fellowship, as well as five grants from the Witter Bynner Foundation for Poetry, Sze was the first poet laureate of Santa Fe, where he lives with his wife, the poet Carol Moldaw. From 2012 to 2017, he was a chancellor of the Academy of American Poets, and in 2017, he was elected a fellow of the American Academy of Arts and Sciences. His poems have been translated into over a dozen languages, including Chinese, Dutch, German, Korean, and Spanish. He is a professor emeritus at the Institute of American Indian Arts.

Lannan Literary Selections

For two decades Lannan Foundation has supported the publication and distribution of exceptional literary works. Copper Canyon Press gratefully acknowledges their support.

LANNAN LITERARY SELECTIONS 2021

Shangyang Fang, *Burying the Mountain*

June Jordan, *The Essential June Jordan*

Laura Kasischke, *Lightning Falls in Love*

Arthur Sze, *The Glass Constellation: New and Collected Poems*

Fernando Valverde (translated by Carolyn Forché), *América*

RECENT LANNAN LITERARY SELECTIONS FROM COPPER CANYON PRESS

Mark Bibbins, *13th Balloon*

Sherwin Bitsui, *Dissolve*

Jericho Brown, *The Tradition*

Victoria Chang, *Obit*

Leila Chatti, *Deluge*

John Freeman, *Maps*

Jenny George, *The Dream of Reason*

Deborah Landau, *Soft Targets*

Rachel McKibbens, *blud*

Philip Metres, *Shrapnel Maps*

Aimee Nezhukumatathil, *Oceanic*

Camille Rankine, *Incorrect Merciful Impulses*

Paisley Rekdal, *Nightingale*

Natalie Scenters-Zapico, *Lima :: Limón*

Natalie Shapero, *Popular Longing*

Frank Stanford, *What About This: Collected Poems of Frank Stanford*

C.D. Wright, *Casting Deep Shade*

Matthew Zapruder, *Father's Day*

Poetry is vital to language and living. Since 1972, Copper Canyon Press has published extraordinary poetry from around the world to engage the imaginations and intellects of readers, writers, booksellers, librarians, teachers, students, and donors.

WE ARE GRATEFUL FOR THE MAJOR SUPPORT PROVIDED BY:

THE PAUL G. ALLEN FAMILY FOUNDATION

amazon *literary partnership*

Lannan

TO LEARN MORE ABOUT UNDERWRITING
COPPER CANYON PRESS TITLES,
PLEASE CALL 360-385-4925 EXT. 103

WE ARE GRATEFUL FOR THE MAJOR SUPPORT PROVIDED BY:

Anonymous
Jill Baker and Jeffrey Bishop
Anne and Geoffrey Barker
In honor of Ida Bauer, Betsy Gifford, and Beverly Sachar
Donna and Matthew Bellew
Will Blythe
John Branch
Diana Broze
John R. Cahill
The Beatrice R. and Joseph A. Coleman Foundation
The Currie Family Fund
Laurie and Oskar Eustis
Austin Evans
Saramel Evans
Mimi Gardner Gates
Gull Industries Inc. on behalf of William True
The Trust of Warren A. Gummow
Carolyn and Robert Hedin
Bruce Kahn
Phil Kovacevich and Eric Wechsler
Lakeside Industries Inc. on behalf of Jeanne Marie Lee
Maureen Lee and Mark Busto
Peter Lewis and Johnna Turiano
Ellie Mathews and Carl Youngmann as The North Press
Hank and Liesel Meijer
Jack Nicholson
Gregg Orr
Petunia Charitable Fund and adviser Elizabeth Hebert
Gay Phinny
Suzanne Rapp and Mark Hamilton
Adam and Lynn Rauch
Emily and Dan Raymond
Jill and Bill Ruckelshaus
Cynthia Sears
Kim and Jeff Seely
Joan F. Woods
Barbara and Charles Wright
Caleb Young as C. Young Creative
The dedicated interns and faithful volunteers of Copper Canyon Press

The Chinese character for poetry is made up of two parts:
"word" and "temple." It also serves as pressmark for
Copper Canyon Press.

The poems are set in Minion Pro.
Book design and composition by Phil Kovacevich.